H6

The Origins
of Capitalism

The Origins
of Capitalism

JEAN BAECHLER

translated by
Barry Cooper

BASIL BLACKWELL · OXFORD

ISBN 0 631 16320 4

Originally published as
Les Origines du capitalisme
© Éditions Gallimard, Paris 1971
and translated by arrangement

Set in Monotype Bembo
Printed in Great Britain
by Western Printing Services Ltd., Bristol
and bound at the Kemp Hall Bindery, Oxford

Contents

For Fabienne

Preface

An earlier version of this study appeared under the title: 'Essai sur les origines du système capitaliste', *Archives européennes de Sociologie*, IX, 2 (1968), pp. 205–63. Friends have been kind enough to suggest that it be removed from this scholarly obscurity and made available to a wider public. I leave responsibility for the initiative with them; the result is my own burden.

I have tried to retain the style of the original essay. First because I find it more congenial than putting together a bulky work, weighed down by notes and digressions. But also because I am convinced that the exercise I have undertaken is possible only in an essay form. The essay is suitable for tackling a very precise problem. One tries to resolve it on the basis of an hypothesis pushed to its ultimate consequences. Nuances and second thoughts are out of place: one must write as if certain of one's knowledge. An essay is not a summary of available information. It is a point of view. This is why no previously unknown facts, no information that could not be gleaned from an ordinary history book, will be found here. My sole ambition has been to deal with these facts in a new light. It is for the reader to say whether it has been pursued in vain. I might add that I consider it justified only if my (probably paradoxical) analysis allows us to reconsider certain scholarly problems on new bases.

The first version was published three years before the book from which this translation was made. Without claiming to have spent the whole intervening period trying to verify my hypotheses, I have, nevertheless, extended my documentation and dealt with certain points in greater depth. As my article had been based almost exclusively upon western historical material, I sought for this book to adduce supplementary proof from non-western civilizations. My first surprise was to note the extent to which a comparative method verified my first hypotheses. However, I have been led to make them more specific, to accentuate certain points, to extend some of my arguments, to make certain supplementary hypotheses more explicit, and to drop some others altogether. I am fully aware that if I gave myself a further few years for reflection, I would manage to alter my text and my argument once again, but, all things considered, I am inclined to believe that the present version has been elaborated and pondered enough to risk publication. Though I am ready to ask the indulgence of the reader for the solution I have given to the problem posed, I am less inclined towards concessions over the method I have followed. To speak plainly, I attach greater importance to the method than to the illustration I have given of it.

I have reduced references and notes to a minimum, and indicated only those works and authors that have been useful to me on precise points. There is nothing confidential about the general historical documentation I have used, and I have not thought it worthwhile to specify references to well-known material.

A note on the translation: Reference has been made to English translations, where they exist, and to standard reference books where supplementary documentation has seemed worthwhile. A few minor errors have been silently corrected.

Introduction

By the breadth of the questions to which they give rise, and from fear of ending up with a grandiose intellectual construction impervious to empirical verification, some historical problems accentuate one's modesty as a theorist and induce us to abandon them. Within western civilization three major changes fall within this shadowy zone of reflection: the advent of the Greek city-state system, the fall of the Western Roman Empire,[1] and above all, the origins of the capitalist system. The explanation for this caution is simple. It belongs to the nature of the historian's way of reasoning, which bases its procedure on an elaboration of intellectual schemata that cut the infinite flux of human societies into isolated units so that these units then may be grasped conceptually. It follows that explanatory systems eventually function well for each unit taken in its particularity (since it is the intellectual system that constitutes its object), but come to grief when dealing with the basic changes that can affect a whole society. In fact, every reflection upon the broadest of historical ensembles (ancient

---

[1] Appearances here are deceptive. The literature on the Late Empire is enormous and the interpretations of the crisis of the Western Empire from the third century on are particularly numerous. However, analyses that deal specifically in the realm of explanations and aspire to a genuine theory are much more rare. The most important effort in this area, in my view, is a short essay by Max Weber, the least known but perhaps the most elegant he wrote: 'Die sozialen Gründe des Untergangs den antiken Kultur', in *Gesammelte Aufsätze zur Sozial- und Wirtschaftsgeschichte* (Tübingen: J. C. B. Mohr, 1924), pp. 289–311. (The essay was originally published in 1896.)

society, western feudalism, etc.), under pain of being lost in the eclectic juxtaposition of partial accounts, is bound to construct and to perceive these ensembles from a unique point of view; every reflection is launched by a process of unilateral development of one of its major aspects (the city, the empire, capitalism, economic under-development etc.). Inevitably upon completing such a process, one ends up building the structure of this ensemble. That is, one ends with a logical system that provides an account of its composite elements and their necessary relations. Now, a structure is necessarily static,[2] even if the analysis allows for the possibilities of variation of any given structure. It follows that radical innovation during the evolution of human societies is placed, by nature and by definition, at the conjunction of two distinct ensembles and that this innovation does not appear and cannot appear within the historian's field of consciousness. By trading qualitative change for quantitative modifications, the problem may be concealed, and so, however little one may have intended to deal with Hegel, it must be done.

Truth to tell, a more prosaic explanation, which does not contradict what has been stated, may be advanced. An intellectual, especially if he is French, is scarcely trained to consider the great configurations of human history. For the historian, the administrative slicing of his discipline obliges him to ensconce himself in a narrow spatio-temporal sector of historiography; what can he possibly say when, professionally, he refuses to retain any hypothesis that is not based upon a document, which automatically eliminates the very questions I would like to raise? For never will a literary, epigraphical, or archaeological document give me an explanation of the origins of the Greek city: such a document can only be generated within the very framework of the city. As for the philosopher, his historical education usually rests upon what he remembers from school. He is limited to a few notions of ancient and contemporary history, just enough to provide materials for a brilliant and useless essay.

Thus, there is no mystery in the fact, which at first seems scandalous, that historiography, whose object of study, in its very essence, is historical evolution, constantly avoids it for want of ability to grasp it in itself. A caricature of this impotence is provided by philosophies of history such as those of Spengler and Toynbee which, having given themselves the whole of history as an object of study, merely end up with

[2] From which follows the necessity for structuralist thought to choose or assume systems in equilibrium.

the juxtaposition of partial and static histories, locked within their radical particularity.

It is not my purpose, in the present work, to pursue further the clarification of this contradiction between a dynamic historical reality and the historian's static conceptualization save to aver that it arises from a paradox of reason, whereby reason considers as radically new or as a chance effect anything for which it cannot account. Having said that, it is always allowable to want to reduce as much as possible the part of the irrational that creeps into every intellectual construction. Besides, I have tried here to focus interest upon a major transformation, the origins of the capitalist system, with the intention of making from this inquiry an outline of a theory of historical evolution. One could formulate the problem to be considered as follows: what results may one hope to achieve when one takes the origins of a total social phenomenon as an object of study? It is not a matter of once again establishing, as so many others have done, the historical facts involved, of re-tracing the major aspects of the evolution of the western economy. Rather, what is involved is a reply not to the how,[3] the when, and the where, but to the *why* of this phenomenon which has governed the destiny of western men for several centuries, and will do so for humanity in the future. To do this I will begin with the theses of a thinker who is most interested in this problem, Marx. Not that I should like to sacrifice to a cult or display any of my own meagre erudition, but because the critique of an already established thought is the most convenient way to arrive at a new statement of the problems.

[3] This is why I have at no time had to use or to criticize the celebrated theses of W. W. Rostow in his *Stages of Economic Growth: A Non-communist Manifesto* (Cambridge: Cambridge University Press, 1960). The most favourable reading of it would be that he *described* the five stages of the economic evolution of humanity; a critical eye will discern in it a reply primarily addressed to vulgar Marxism. In any case, there is not a word about the problem I am concerned with.

Part One
Marx's Theory

During the course of his intellectual career, Marx entered upon the subject of the origins of the capitalist system several times. Three texts analyse the problem at length: The German Ideology, *the* Foundations of the Critique of Political Economy, *and* Capital. *The solutions offered in each text are sufficiently divergent to justify separate analyses.*

One: *The German Ideology*[1]

In a single presumptuous overview Marx considered the economic evolution of the West from the Middle Ages or, more precisely, from the eleventh century. In this way he distinguished three great stages that have led to contemporary capitalism:

1. The first is characterized, and was initiated, by the separation of town and country. From this initial break, everything became possible —or rather, became necessary: 'The existence of the town implies, at the same time, the necessity of administration, police, taxes, etc., in short, of the municipality, and thus of politics in general' (pp. 43-4). This separation reveals other original relations between men as well: 'The antagonism of town and country can only exist as a result of private property. It is the most gross expression of the subjection of the individual under the division of labour, under a definite activity imposed upon him' (p. 44). And finally, 'the separation of town and country can also be understood as the separation of capital and landed property, as the beginning of the existence and development of capital independent of landed property—the beginning of property having its basis only in labour and exchange' (p. 44). In short, the separation of town and country is accompanied by three phenomena organically

---

1 *The German Ideology*, ed. B. Pascal (London: Lawrence and Wishart, 1938); *The Grundrisse: Foundations of the Critique of Political Economy*, tr. M. Nicolaus (Harmondsworth: Penguin, 1973); *Capital*, vol. I, tr. S. Moore and E. Aveling (New York: International Publishers, 1967). References in the text are to these editions.

connected with it: (a) the appearance of the political sphere; (b) the division of labour and the constitution of the economic sphere, external to, and coercive of, the individual; (c) the birth of industrial and commercial capital alongside landed property.

Symmetrically, medieval cities were populated by fugitive serfs who entered them to all intents and purposes with nothing but the strength of their arms and whatever vocational skills they chanced to possess. 'The conflict among the interests of the various crafts, the necessity of protecting their laboriously acquired skill, and the feudal organization of the whole of the country: these were the causes of the union of the workers of each craft in guilds' (p. 45). Serfs continued to flee manorial exploitation but now found themselves confronting constituted guilds, closed shops that denied them entry. In consequence, they had to be satisfied with becoming day-labourers pure and simple, so that 'the need for day-labourers in the towns created the rabble' (p. 45).

This is all very primitive and embryonic, for the limited extent of commerce prevented the appearance of money-capital. 'Capital in these towns was a natural capital, consisting of a house, the tools of the craft, and the natural, hereditary customers; and not being realizable, on account of the backwardness of commerce and the lack of circulation, it descended from father to son. Unlike modern capital, which can be assessed in money and which may be indifferently invested in this thing or that, this capital was directly connected with the particular work of the owner, inseparable from it and to this extent 'estate [i.e., *standisches*] capital' (p. 47).

A further extension of the division of labour was attained when production and commerce were separated. This meant: (a) the appearance of a specific class of merchants; (b) an increase in public security and commercial communications in keeping with the constitution of political units and the ability of a central authority to impose its writ; (c) an increase in the needs and resources within the region considered; (d) division of labour *between* towns: 'The local restrictions of earlier times begin gradually to be broken down' (p. 48); (e) 'In the Middle Ages the citizens in each town were compelled to unite against the landed nobility to save their skins. The extension of trade, the establishment of communications, led the separate towns to get to know other towns, which had asserted the same interests in the struggle with the same antagonist. Out of the many local corporations of burghers there arose only gradually the bourgeois *class*' (p. 48).

This division of labour culminated in the establishment of the first manufacturers, which were outside the guild system. Manufacture was based upon three conditions: (a) an already well developed international trade; (b) an already increasing concentration of population; (c) a similar concentration of capital. Manufacture prospered first of all with textiles, a sector of industry where the division of labour is developed most naturally and where the machine can be most easily introduced: 'Weaving, an occupation demanding in most cases little skill and soon splitting up into countless branches, by its whole nature resisted the trammels of the guild. Weaving was therefore carried on mostly in villages and market-centres without guild organization, which gradually became towns, and indeed the most flourishing towns in each land' (pp. 50–1). Thus, the genesis of capitalism, beyond the simple accumulation of capital that every social order presupposes, is connected on the one hand to the appearance of moveable capital, capital that can be turned into money, and on the other to manufacture whose formation the above texts seem to suggest followed from the nature of the textile industry. In its turn, manufacture leads to two essential consequences: first, struggles among nations become commercial struggles, 'trade had from now on a political significance' (p. 52); and second, relations between labourers and capitalists became money relations.

Neither the discovery of America nor colonization followed from the general economic movement. It was an autonomous (and unexplained) phenomenon, which had important repercussions for economic development owing to the appearance of a world market and the introduction of considerable masses of gold and silver into circulation. This rapid expansion of trade, and thus of production, had socially important consequences: 'trade and manufacture created the big bourgeoisie: in the guilds was concentrated the petty bourgeoisie, which no longer was dominant in the towns as formerly, but had to bow to the decline of the guilds, as soon as they came into contact with manufacture' (p. 53).

2. 'The second period began in the middle of the seventeenth century and lasted almost to the end of the eighteenth' (p. 54). It was characterized by an overwhelming preponderance of large-scale international and colonial commerce. Manufacturing had only a subordinate role. Large-scale commerce was based upon the restriction of competition through protective tariffs, prohibitions, and treaties of the sort that 'in the last resort, competition was carried on and decided by wars

(especially naval wars)' (p. 54). England emerged victorious from this struggle and found itself at the centre of world commerce.

But this stage was also marked by a new transformation of the nature of capital. Here the monetary aspect was accentuated: 'This period is also characterized by the cessation of the bans on the export of gold and silver and the beginning of the bullion trade, by banks, national debts, paper money, by speculation in stocks and shares and stock-jobbing in all articles, by the development of finance in general. Again capital lost a great part of the natural character which had clung to it' (pp. 55–6).

3. The third stage was ushered in by the appearance of large-scale industry and mechanization. It was tied directly to the preceding stage. In fact, the commercial preponderance of England led to a massive demand for English products that the apparatus of production was unable to satisfy. In response to this demand, the forces of production were overturned, the other necessary conditions, 'freedom of competition inside the nation, the development of theoretical mechanics, etc.' (p. 56), having already been established by other means. From England the industrial revolution necessarily moved on to other countries: 'Competition soon compelled every country that wished to retain its historical role to protect its manufactures by renewed customs regulations (the old duties were no longer any good against big industry), and soon afterwards to introduce big industry under protective duties' (p. 56).

From this time on the modern industrial system has established its position. It is characterized, *inter alia*, by: (a) the creation of a world market that governs both nations and individuals; (b) the resolution 'of all natural relationships into money relationships'; (c) the creation of large industrial cities, the destruction of artisans and crafts and 'the victory of the commercial town over the countryside' (p. 57); (d) the appearance for the first time of a class that was by nature international, 'a class which is really rid of all the old world and at the same time stands pitted against it' (p. 57).

If one tries to reduce the argument to its essential structure, the explanation may be seen to rest on the following points: (a) the separation of town and country; (b) the appearance of a commercial social group; (c) the extension of commercial relations over an ever-increasing area; (d) the appearance of manufacture; (e) the extension of commerce over the whole world because of the discovery of America and colonization; (f) the domination of the world market by a single nation, England; (g) the development of the forces of production so as to respond to an ever increasing demand. All this led to the industrial revolution.

First of all, this explanation gives us information about Marx's central intuition during this time (1845–6) when, along with Engels, he was writing *The German Ideology*. In fact, what is astonishing is the great importance attributed to the creation of a world market and the assertion that each stage in the development of capitalism is found to be tied to an extension of the market. The intolerable thing is precisely the existence of a market that escapes the control of men, who then become simple and inarticulate puppets in the hands of this blind power. The end of this outrage consists in the conscious control of the market by humanity, and the means for ending the invidious destiny of the market is to be the proletariat. Consequently, every reflection on the origins of the capitalist system is centred upon the movement from a closed village economy to a world market. This point lays bare a rule of first importance for all history that seeks to account for origins, a rule to which I shall have to revert: every effort at explanation rests entirely upon the definition given to the phenomena to be explained. It follows from this that, according to the specific aspects of the phenomenon that are deemed important, the line of argument will choose from the mass of available historical facts those which appear to confirm the genesis of the phenomenon studied, *as it has been defined*. And as a corollary, every procedure of this kind is necessarily regressive. The infinite mass of facts that constitute the past of a general historical phenomenon is, by itself, undifferentiated, which means that none of the facts can claim a causal priority. It is the historian who introduces a meaning-giving hierarchy into this mass by deciding that such and such a fact or group of facts is pertinent to the phenomenon to be explained. Now, such a procedure is possible only after the fully developed phenomenon has been defined. Consequently, it is a definition of the present and of it alone that allows us to construct the past and to distinguish in it cleavages or lines of force that lead to the present. In principle therefore, a procedure of this kind always has an arbitrary, not to say tautological, character, which seems to me to derive from the paradoxical nature of historians' reasoning.

Having said that we may ask: to what extent is Marx's explanation acceptable? It seems to me to be wrong on two counts: (a) In detail, each of the thresholds that separate one stage from another remains unexplained. Why does one move from village to town? Why do commercial relations expand? Why does one arrive at a world market? None of these fundamental questions receives a reply. In other words, it is not an explanation but a description that wishes to be self-explanatory. (b) Most importantly, other societies and other times have known an evolution of the same type but they did not result in an industrial revolution: the transformation from the Greek city to the Hellenistic empire, the unification of the Mediterranean basin by the Romans, the constitution of a Chinese empire. Cities, merchants, capital, a 'world' market can be found anywhere. But nowhere can be found the leap from an economy based upon agricultural production and limited trade of surplus products to an economy characterized by a massive increase in production and constant diversification. Consequently, in spite of all the seductive coherence of the Marxian argument (which is to say nothing of the quality of the information employed, remarkable as it is considering the state of medieval historiography during the time that Marx's text was written), it does not achieve its goal since it has not been applied to the task of sifting out the original aspects of Western economic evolution. This allows us to make more precise the earlier remark dealing with the rules of all history seeking to account for origins. In the ultimately adopted definition of the phenomena whose origins one intends to pursue, the utmost care must be given to noting what constitutes its specific features. This can only be done if one has proceeded beforehand to determine the differences that distinguish it from other observable systems. In turn, these differences only crop up if the different objects that constitute the class studied (in this case, economic systems) are tested by appropriate criteria. Consequently, in searching for the particularities of western destiny that can help me to explain its originality, my first task will be to elucidate the unique characteristics of the Western economic system.

Two: *The Grundrisse*

During the years following the writing of this work of his youth, Marx applied himself, as is well-known, to the elaboration of his major works in economics. His entire effort was directed precisely towards determining the specific features of the capitalist system. This ambition was stated forcefully in the methodological section of the 'Introduction' to the *Grundrisse* (pp. 100–8), and in particular in the following passage: 'In all forms of society there is one specific kind of production which predominates over the rest, whose relations thus assign rank and influence to the others. It is a general illumination which bathes all the other colours and modifies their particularity. It is a particular ether which determines the specific gravity of every being which has materialized within it' (pp. 106–7). Thus, one may hope for a more substantial reply than has been received so far to the problem that we are dealing with at the moment. Let us consider first of all the view developed in the *Grundrisse*, the *Foundations of the Critique of Political Economy* (1857–8). This work remained in manuscript form, never having been revised nor corrected, but was entirely recast as *Capital*. Nevertheless, nearly all the fundamental theses of *Capital* can be found in it. Some lengthy passages are devoted to my problem, but they have been loosely written, the way one fills notebooks; so much so that the development of Marx's ideas is not always so rigorous as to suggest the presentation given to them here.

The essence of capitalism is found in the confrontation of capital and labour-power.[2] An exchange is produced between the two, and this

[2] Marx will generally use this expression in *Capital* in preference to labour,

exchange lays the basis for capitalism. Here is a particularly clear quotation:

> The *use value* which confronts capital as posited exchange value is *labour*. Capital exchanges itself, or exists in this role, only in connection with *not-capital*, the negation of capital, without which it is not capital; the real *not-capital* is *labour*.
>
> If we consider the exchange between capital and labour, then we find that it splits into two processes which are not only formally but also qualitatively different, and even contradictory:
>
> (1) The worker sells his commodity, labour, which has a use value, and, as a commodity, also a *price*, like all other commodities, for a specific sum of exchange values, specific sum of money, which capital concedes to him.
>
> (2) The capitalist obtains labour itself, labour as value-positing activity, as productive labour; i.e. he obtains the productive force which maintains and multiplies capital, and which thereby becomes the productive force, the reproductive force of capital, a force belonging to capital itself.
>
> The separation of these two processes is so obvious that they can take place at different times, and need by no means coincide. The first process can be and usually, to a certain extent, is completed before the second even begins. The completion of the second act presupposes the completion of the product. The payment of wages cannot wait for that. We will even find it an essential aspect of the relation, that it does not wait for that (p. 274).

One might multiply the citations, but they all head in the same direction: what radically distinguishes the capitalist system from all other modes of production is wage-labour, that is to say, the fact that certain men can buy not the results of labour but the labour-power of other men. This exchange is unequal, for the capitalist pays out only the goods necessary for the preservation and reproduction of labour-power (the value of all of this is maintained by the worker and imparted to production during a fraction of the labouring day, what Marx will call necessary labour), but he uses labour-power beyond necessary labour, so that labour imparts to production a value greater than that

which he employs in the *Grundrisse*; labour is too vague a term since it can designate equally the labour-power of an individual (latent labour), the employment of this power (effective labour), or its results (works).

which would correspond to the simple replacement of necessary labour (what Marx calls surplus-value). Consequently the problem of the origins of capitalism may be framed in the following terms: what events ended with some men, men who had money in hand, finding labour-power available in the market?[3]

As I have shown, the only possible explanation is regressive. It may take two different forms, focussing upon: (a) the origin of capital, which is the problem of primitive accumulation; or (b) the origin of labour-power, which is the problem of the expropriation of labourers, peasants, and artisans.

On the first point, Marx immediately gets into difficulty and contents himself with a few general remarks that do nothing but argue the real problem away.

The conditions and presuppositions of *becoming*, of the *arising*, of capital presuppose precisely that it is not yet in being but merely in *becoming*; they therefore disappear as real capital arises, capital which itself, on the basis of its own reality, points the conditions for its realization. Thus e.g. while the process in which money or value for-itself originally becomes capital presupposes on the part of the capitalist an accumulation—perhaps by means of savings garnered from products and values created by his own labour etc., which he has undertaken as a *not-capitalist*, i.e., while the presuppositions under which money becomes capital appear as given, external *presuppositions* for the arising of capital—nevertheless, as soon as capital has become capital as such, it creates its own presuppositions, i.e. the possession of the real conditions of the creation of new values *without exchange*—by means of its own production process (pp. 459–60).

In short, when capitalist relations are established, the problem of their origin is posed no longer; beforehand, every sum of money whatever its genesis, can become capital. But the transformation of the one into

[3] The question concerning the origins of surplus-value has not been asked. In effect, the fact that the value conferred upon an object is not fully paid over to the worker is coeval with capitalism. Surplus-value effectively constitutes the sole source whereby the entrepreneur, the financier, and the real estate owner increase their profits, interest, and rent. In the absence of surplus-value, the three categories of capitalists would have no reason to devote themselves to economic activity, since then they would do nothing but return to the economic system the exact equivalent of what they took out. Consequently, as soon as capitalism is a datum, so is surplus-value. Properly speaking, therefore, it has no distinct origin.

the other is completely ignored. Here we have a perfect illustration of the paradox I suggested in the introduction: when one is placed in a determined system, considered as an orderly and necessary arrangement of necessary elements, it is as impossible to account for the arrangement as it is to account for the elements that make it up. Necessarily one ends up with a tautology: money becomes capital within the framework of the capitalist system. Marx seems to have had an intimation of the dilemma even while postponing the solution for a later work:

On the other side, much more important for us is that our method indicates the points where historical investigation must enter in, or where bourgeois economy as a merely historical form of the production process points beyond itself to earlier historical modes of production. In order to develop the laws of bourgeois economy, therefore, it is not necessary to write the *real history of the relations of production*. But the correct observation and deduction of these laws, as having themselves become in history, always leads to primary equations—like the empirical numbers e.g. in natural science—which point towards a past lying behind this system. These indications, together with a correct grasp of the present, then also offer the key to the understanding of the past—a work in its own right which, it is to be hoped, we shall be able to undertake as well (pp. 460-1).

In a letter to Lasalle, dated 22 February 1858, Marx took up this last point again and told his correspondent of his intention to write three parallel works: (a) a critique of the capitalist system, which was to be *Capital*; (b) a critique of bourgeois political economy of which something more than the outlines can be found in *A Contribution to The Critique of Political Economy* (1859), in several passages of *Capital*, and in his posthumous work, *Theories of Surplus-Value*; (c) an historical outline of economic relations or categories.

This last work was never completed, nor even begun, which may legitimately be explained by a lack of time or by the fact that his own presuppositions reduced the usefulness of such an exercise to nothing. All he would have succeeded in doing would have been to achieve the *juxtaposition* of historical modes of production, and not a reasoned account of the transformation of one mode into another. As proof I should like to cite only the following passage, where Marx inextricably entangles himself in contradictions:

However, if we consider the original relation, before the entry of money into the self-realization process, then various conditions appear which have to have arisen, or been given historically, for money to become capital and labour to become capital-positing, capital-creating labour, wage labour. . . . The essential conditions are themselves posited in the relation as it appears originally: (a) on the one side the presence of living labour-power as a merely *subjective* existence, separated from the *conditions* of living labour as well as from the *means of existence, the necessary goods*, the means of self-preservation of *labour-power*; the living possibility of labour, on the one side, in this complete abstraction; (b) the value, or objectified labour, found on the other side, must be an accumulation of use values sufficiently large to furnish the objective conditions ont only for the production of the products or values required to reproduce or maintain living labour-power, but also for the absorption of surplus labour—to supply the objective material for the latter; (c) a free exchange—money circulation—between both sides; between the extremes a relation founded on exchange values—not on the master-servant relation—i.e., hence, production which does not directly furnish the producer with his necessaries, but which is mediated through exchange, and which cannot therefore usurp alien labour directly, but must buy it, exchange it, from the worker himself; finally, (d) one side—the side representing the objective conditions of labour in the form of independent values for—themselves—must present itself as *value*, and must regard the positing of values, self-realization, money-making, as the ultimate purpose—not direct consumption or the creation of use value (pp. 463–4).

It is quite plain that these four conditions are not external to the capitalist system as Marx has defined it but represent simple elaborations of his own definition. Thus they do nothing to resolve the problem posed. The last point, which indicates what could be called the spirit of capitalism, is particularly eloquent: it is not an external condition of the capitalist system that might aid us in clarifying its origins, but a presupposition belonging to its very essence.

Thus it is that the birth of capital remains mysterious for us. Let us see the genesis of the second element in capitalism, the free labourer.

So that the free labourer could appear the following conditions were necessary: (a) 'the *dissolution* of the relation to the earth—land and soil—as the natural condition of production' (p. 497), a relation that is woven from within a community or commune; (b) *'dissolution of the relations in which man appears as proprietor of the instrument'* of labour (p. 497), such as the medieval artisan; (c) that the labourer did not possess the means necessary to survive during the time it takes a given process of production to be completed. In other words, the labourer must be deprived of any reserve consumption fund (pp. 497-8). (d) *'Dissolution* likewise at the same time of the relations in which the *workers themselves*, the *living labour-power*, still belong *directly among the objective conditions of production*, and are appropriated as such—i.e. are slaves or serfs' (p. 498).

These successive dissolutions have their symmetrical correspondence in the realm of ownership and property, which undergoes the following transformations: an end to real estate or landed property as a sole source of wealth; an end to ownership of the instruments of labour, which were created by labour itself; an end to ownership of the means of subsistence that are tied neither to property, nor the land, nor to tools. Clearly, what this means is that the labourer is deprived of any reserve, whereas, by contrast, the slave or serf was fed, housed, and clothed.[4] Consequently, these are all double dissolutions: the process that leads to the constitution of free labourers simultaneously results in the freeing of the means of production. Only under this condition does capital, in its monetary form, find at the same time in the market and in free labour its own necessary conditions for existence.

Thus one finds three conjoint processes: the development of monetary wealth, the production of the free labourer and the freeing of the means of production. These three processes are dialectually related:

It goes without saying—and shows itself if we go more deeply into the historic epoch under discussion here—that in truth the *period of dissolution* of the earlier modes of production and modes of the worker's relation to the objective conditions of labour *is at the same time a period* in which *monetary wealth* on the one side *has* already developed to a certain extent, and on the other side grows and expands rapidly through the same circumstances as accelerate the above dissolution. It is itself one of the agencies of that dissolution,

[4] We must admit that a certain amount of subtlety is required to see a kind of ownership in this instance. Generally speaking, all these pages are a kind of Hegelian parody, which is irritating for the reader and does violence to the subject-matter by creating artificial symmetries.

while at the same time that dissolution is the condition of its transformation into capital (p. 506).

The concluding phrase is particularly symptomatic of the contradictions that Marx struggles with: in order for there to be capitalism these three processes are necessary, but they only appear within the womb of the capitalist system. One may consider in turn each of the dissolutions that Marx reveals, and none is explained save by the addition of our unknown additional factor, a mysterious power that is nothing but capitalism itself. It would have been better to try and grasp these processes in their earliest aspects, in their incipient state. Marx explains nothing about where these processes came from, but simply notes or supposes that they exist. Here again Marx is aware of the difficulty, since he writes:

But the *mere presence of monetary wealth*, and even the achievement of a kind of supremacy on its part, is in no way sufficient for this *dissolution into capital* to happen. Or else ancient Rome, Byzantium etc. would have ended their history with free labour and capital, or rather begun a new history. There, too, the dissolution of the old property relations was bound up with the development of monetary wealth—of trade etc. But instead of leading to industry, this dissolution in fact led to the supremacy of the countryside over the city (p. 506).

What is (or are) the factor (or factors) that explain the divergence of evolutions? No answer can be found in the *Grundrisse*. Perhaps we may find it in *Capital*.

Three: *Capital*

The *Grundrisse*, despite its title, is much more than a rough draft for *Capital*. All the essential ideas of the later work are found in it (even if the central concepts of constant capital and variable capital are not found in it, their content is). In fact, *Capital* appears as the definitive, closed, and systematic edition of what Marx had written for himself in the *Grundrisse* in order to assure himself that he had something worthwhile to say. The problem that I am concerned with is dealt with in Part VIII, 'The So-called Primitive Accumulation'. Here his exposition is much more clear and precise, and has been rid of all the Hegelian pastiche. And most importantly, he introduces a number of interesting novelties.

The capitalist system is once again defined as the purchase by monetary capital of free labour-power that in turn produces more value than is given to it in wages. The defining trait of the system is thus wage-labour that, in order to exist, endure, and expand, necessarily is based upon the divorce that has occurred between the labourer and the means of production (land and implements). And wage-labour falls into the hands of the capitalist.

The second moment of this process: the labourer must be able to sell his labour-power where he pleases; the dissolution of service ties and the corporate feudal hierarchy places him in this situation. This dissolution has freed him, but at the same time removed all guarantees of interdependence such as were assured by previous social ties. The labourer is not just free to sell his labour-power, he can not do otherwise.

The third moment is the capitalist entrepreneur. It is necessary for him to carve out a place in the face of opposition from the guild-craftsmen and the landed aristocracy. To attain his own ends, he will, in fact, employ indirect means above all others, turning to his own benefit every event that is going in his direction. 'The knights of industry, however, only succeed in supplanting the knights of the sword by making use of events of which they themselves were wholly innocent. They have risen by means as vile as those by which the Roman freedman once on a time made himself the master of his patronus' (p. 715).

That is all very well and good, but it is hardly satisfactory. For two things are made one: *either* these three processes are connected and, in this case, they can crop up only within the framework of the capitalist system. But then they no more explain its genesis here than they do in the *Grundrisse*. *Or*, they are mutually independent but have been completed by being joined to each other; in this case, the birth of capitalism is the result of pure chance, a conjunction of several series of causes, a conjunction that, in other respects, is altogether highly improbable. Either way, it is an admission of defeat: the problem of the origin of capitalism falls outside the field covered by Marx's intellectual system.

The second horn of the dilemma certainly preoccupies Marx. 'In the history of primitive accumulation, all revolutions are epoch-making that act as levers for the capitalist class in course of formation; but, above all, those moments when great masses of men are suddenly and forcibly torn from their means of subsistence, and hurled as free and "unattached" proletarians on the labour-market' (p. 716). Marx's inability to grasp the origin of capitalism is logically translated into the chronological slicing of Western history: while in *The German Ideology* and the *Grundrisse*, Marx rightly traced the problem back to the eleventh century, *Capital* has capitalism begin in the sixteenth century: 'Although we come across the first beginnings of capitalist production as early as the fourteenth or fifteenth century, sporadically, in certain towns of the Mediterranean, *the capitalist era dates from the sixteenth century*. Wherever it appears, the abolition of serfdom has long been effected, and the highest development of the middle ages, the existence of sovereign towns, has long been on the wane' (pp. 715–16). His choice of a date is perfectly arbitrary; but that is unimportant: what is essential is that Marx no longer envisaged the genesis of capitalism but its adult state. The whole problem of its origins is suggested and conjured away in the phrase, 'wherever it appears. . . .' This passage alone tends to suggest that Marx has given up upon constructing a general theory of historical evolution in order to concentrate upon one determined stage of this evolution.

Having given up examining the first steps of the capitalist system, all Marx's attention was centred on the birth of manufacturing and then of large-scale industry. In fact, by introducing some additional and very interesting details, he rediscovered certain problems outlined in *The German Ideology*. I must confine myself to a consideration of the essential structure of his argument, for to follow Marx into detail would simply encumber the exposition. His argument develops in two directions:

1. *An explanation of the expropriation of the rural population and the genesis of the capitalist farmer*. The phenomenon rests upon the bloody scourge of violence and extortion, and upon State intervention on behalf of property-owners. But why was Marx so interested in these phenomena of rural expropriation?[5] First of all because he needed an uninterrupted and forced production of free labour. But mostly because he had to dissolve the economy of peasant autarchy so as to create an internal market since, in fact, up to this time, the goods produced in rural areas were for the most part directly consumed by their producers without having to pass through the intermediary of a market. From now on they were to be sold in bulk to commercial middle-men. Likewise, all the objects that peasants formerly made domestically (essentially textiles) were henceforth to be produced by industrial manufacture. 'Thus, hand in hand with the expropriation of the self-supporting peasants and their transformation into wage-labourers, with their separation from their means of production, goes the destruction of rural domestic industry, the process of separation between manufacture and agriculture' (p. 748). In fact, this divorce is completed with the appearance of large-scale industry.

This whole explanation is somewhat less than convincing.[6] The expropriation of peasants could tempt the land-owning farmers only

[5] According to all the evidence, Marx over-estimated their importance. All the agrarian history recounted in Chapters Twenty-seven and Twenty-eight of Part Eight of *Capital* is English. Nothing of the kind can be found in France, Belgium, Germany or northern Italy, and these areas have had no major difficulty in receiving the industrial revolution.

[6] Obviously I am leaving aside all criticism sustained by developments outside of historiography so as to deal more closely with the logical incoherence of the argument.

because their profits were a result of land exploitation. Now, these profits presuppose the existence of a market where produce can be disposed of; thus, it is not the farm that created the market but the other way around. Consequently, the evolution of agriculture, as it has been described by Marx, is possible only within the framework of the new mode of production. On the other hand, the annihilation of rural industry does not necessarily proceed from the transformation of peasants into wage-labourers: these two phenomena have no direct connection. On the contrary, it is because industrial manufacturing and then large-scale industry produced goods more cheaply that rural industry was doomed.

2. *The genesis of industrial capital.* This is already a complex matter without Marx having to introduce a hierarchy into the factors he considers. (a) In the beginning there is capital formed by commerce. There is nothing particularly Western about this as it is found in most economic regimes (p. 751). (b) These kinds of capital become industrial capital. In order to overcome the obstacles of a feudal constitution and the system of guild corporations, 'the new manufacturers were established at sea-ports, or at inland points beyond the control of the old municipalities and their guilds' (p. 751). Once again we may note that the essential fact, the qualitative leap to industrial capital, is conjured away. (c) The discovery of America and its precious metals, colonization, the slave-trade, and then the mercantile wars (which continued up to the Opium Wars of the 1840's) are the second source of accumulation. Unfortunately for an explanation of the genesis of the system, all these methods of accumulation are not external to it but rather are only its manifestations. Marx affirms this expressly a bit further on: 'Today industrial supremacy implies commercial supremacy. In the period of manufacture properly so called, it is, on the other hand, the commercial supremacy that gives industrial predominance. Hence the preponderant role that the colonial system plays at that time' (p. 754). (d) It is advisable to note, however, an essential notion from this same passage to which I shall have occasion to revert:

These methods of accumulation depend in part upon brute force, e.g. the colonial system. But they all employ the power of the State, the concentrated and organized force of society, to hasten hothouse fashion, the process of transformation of the feudal mode of production into the capitalist mode, and to shorten the transition. *Force is the midwife of every old society pregnant with a new one. Force is itself an economic power* (p. 751).

This is a rather inspired remark, and considering how little Marx developed it, it has led to important conclusions. Now, these words of Marx remained but a marginal observation, and for good reason: the Marxian intellectual system, a philosophy of totality that makes everything rest upon an economic footing, prohibits consideration of the various dimensions of human activity, and in particular the political dimension, as autonomous. From this fact, in developing his remark it would have been necessary to establish that 'in the final analysis' politics depends upon economics, that the modern State is the expression of the capitalist system, and that, consequently, the State cannot explain its birth. An appeal to the subtleties of the dialectic would be vain: we will be left within the confines of tautology or else must avoid the whole problem. (e) Some additional non-economic factors are introduced in the remainder of Marx's exposition, but all are little developed.

> The public debt becomes one of the most powerful levers of primitive accumulation. . . . It has given rise to joint-stock companies, to dealings in negotiable effects of all kinds, and to agiotage, in a word to stock-exchange gambling and the modern bankocracy (pp. 754-5).

> The system of protection was an artificial means of manufacturing manufacturers, of expropriating independent labourers, of capitalizing the national means of production and subsistence, of forcibly abbreviating the transition from the medieval to the modern mode of production (pp. 756-7).

To summarize these pages, written on the basis of a deep and wide-ranging knowledge and in a style both brilliant and stirring, for it was carried along by a prophet's indignation ('capital comes into the world dripping from head and foot, from every pore, with blood and dirt', p. 760), it must be said that Marx returned to a kind of explanation that he had suggested in *The German Ideology*, an explanation by stages. From capital in the form of usury and commerce we move on to industrial capital, which in turn is transformed into commercial capital thanks to the creation of a world market; in order to meet these greatly enlarged economic opportunities, industrial capital arose and henceforth dominates exclusively. But the passage from one stage to another is not explained in spite of Marx's vague awareness of the importance of the State. In short, Marx has not succeeded in escaping from the circle within which he enclosed himself by defining capitalism in terms of the system of wage-labour. The concluding phrase of the first volume of *Capital* forcibly reaffirms this: 'the capitalist mode of production and accumulation, and therefore capitalist private property, have for their fundamental condition the annihilation of self-earned private property; in other words, the expropriation of the labourer' (p. 774). The basis of the system is a part of the system; thus it cannot constitute its foundation.

Here we touch upon a major defect of all Marxian and Marxist constructions. It is presented as a system of total explanation; so as not to go round in circles or bite its own tail, a philosophy of totality necessarily gives greater value to one sector of human activity, which it makes the foundation of the system. Now, there would be a logical contradiction if the foundation were not itself made part of the system and thus were not its own foundation. Throughout this analysis we have run into this dilemma: the origin of the capitalist system presupposes the capitalist system. To express myself in Platonic terms, I would say that the problem of origins is insoluble so long as one considers that Same engenders Same (the economic engenders the economic, the political, the political, the technical, the technical, and so on). I will try to show that we may obtain more satisfactory results by starting from the hypothesis that the Same is engendered by the Other.

To conclude our consideration of Marx and Marxism, let us take note of the paradox of a system that, on the one hand, is presented as a philosophy of history and bases every explanation upon historical evolution and the particularity of historical stages, and that, on the other, runs into difficulties over the impossibility of constructing a theory of origins and, from this fact, is self-refuting. The handicap is rationally insurmountable. This no doubt explains why, from Engels on, there have been attempts to overcome it irrationally. The only way to get around the problem is to create or assume the fiction of an historical foundation that is external to history. The notion of evolution serves precisely this function. Thus, while Marx was content to *record* (and thereby attest implicitly to the impossibility of constructing a theory of history) the succession of primitive communism, slavery, serfdom, oriental despotism, capitalism and so on, his heirs apparent have imagined a necessary evolution. Not that they have been wrong to do so or that they were stupid, because a place for such a law of evolution was necessarily inscribed in the blueprint of this sort of an intellectual system, just as in the periodic table of Mendeleyev places were left for elements that were only later discovered or created. At first sight, Marx's thought is bound to appear paradoxical but in the end it is logical: his was a thought that wished to be historical but, in order to remain coherent, saw itself obliged to eliminate history by establishing itself upon a non-historical principle, the principle of evolution.

Part Two
What is Capitalism?

It would be tempting to submit Max Weber's conception to the same kind of critical analysis as I have just done with Marx's theses. Unfortunately, such a step is impossible. In fact, a Weberian explanation of the origins of capitalism does not exist—or rather, it is multiple. Depending upon whether one follows The Protestant Ethic and the Spirit of Capitalism, Economy and Society, *or the* General Economic History,[1] *the perspectives are different.*

For Weber, capitalism is not, in fact, a single thing but is multiform: in it is expressed most of what makes Western civilization radically original, namely the rationalization of human activities. Thus it would be vain to try to grasp so broad a concept by a simple definition, for it could only be distorted. Thus it is that, for Weber, wage-labour is essential to capitalism. Here he agrees easily enough with Marx. But wage-labour does not exhaust the essence of capitalism. In consequence, the problem of the origin of the system was not really considered. It exists even less saliently in a general way, as Weber was but slightly concerned with problems of historical evolution. Not that this relative indifference was the result of an initial choice (Weber was a thorough historian), but that, because of his method, such matters could only be left in the shade. In fact, the constant determination of original forms by his method of ideal types led him to consider historical objects in their full historical flowering and not just as a temporary or progressive blossom. His best known work, The Protestant Ethic and the Spirit of Capitalism *is in no way a*

---

[1] References are to *The Protestant Ethic and the Spirit of Capitalism*, tr. T. Parsons (London: George Allen & Unwin, 1930); page numbers are found in the text. The parts of *Economy and Society* and the *General Economic History* that have been published separately are noted below at the appropriate places.

theory of the emergence of capitalism from a basis in Protestantism. He tried to show that the Protestant ethic is a form of the rationalization of moral life. Now, capitalism is characterized, according to him, by a rationalization of economic activities: he draws conclusions from this and shows that Protestantism is one of the currents that has contributed to the expansion of capitalism and that it has influenced certain aspects of Western capitalism. In a word, without Protestantism, there still would have been capitalism, but it would have been different. If this interpretation of Weber's argument is accepted, most of the controversy, which his essay has for decades sustained, is found to be beside the point.[2] Having said that, one must add that his analyses, taken individually, are splendid. As a whole, however, they do not provide us with the general picture; instead, each one gives us a particular outline. The general picture is what I propose to deal with here by pointing out, in its proper context, every proposition that confirms the direction of Weber's analyses.

[2] The principal elements of this controversy have been conveniently assembled by Philippe Bernard, *Protestantisme et capitalisme: La controverse post-webérienne* (Paris: Colin, 1970), and by Robert W. Green, *Protestantism and Capitalism: The Weber Thesis and Its Critics* (Boston: Heath, 1959). Both contain extensive bibliographies.

Four: *False Trails*

Before entering at large upon our subject it is important to settle certain problems of terminology. I do not make, nor shall I make here, any distinction between the expressions 'capitalist system' or 'capitalism' and 'industrial system', and we shall see why. As for the expression 'socialist system' or 'socialism', I confess to be ignorant of any adequate usage of the term. If the economic system as is practised in the U.S.S.R. and the Peoples' Democracies is what is meant, I am inclined to see there, *on the economic level*, an aberrant and inefficacious usage: what we are dealing with is a kind of chimera born from the writings of ideologues who have claimed and still claim to construct an economy in systematic ignorance of the laws of economics. If, on the other hand, one means by socialism a type of society radically different from our own and from other known societies, the very most that is involved (for the moment) is only a matter of aspiration; its origins may be a problem for our children's grandchildren, the day it is realized.

The determination of the essence of an historical phenomenon always carries with it a greater or lesser element of arbitrariness, which obliges the understanding to conduct a whole series of precise surgical operations so that the phenomenon may burst forth unencumbered by any inessential additions. Nevertheless, it is possible to limit the arbitrary element by following certain methodological rules. In the first place, we need not take account of all of what Marx placed in the category of 'conditions for capitalism', which is to say, the whole of what is supposed to be given *before* the phenomenon of capitalism may be said to exist. In fact, it is generally impossible to decide whether the condition is the cause or consequence. Let us consider the example of agriculture. Industrialization follows[3] from it: the nineteenth-century industrial revolution was made possible only thanks to progress in cultivation begun in the eighteenth century and completed in the nineteenth. And this was so for two reasons: first because an increase in *per capita* productivity was necessary in order to allow an intense rural exodus without at the same time affecting adversely the general level of nourishment. Secondly, it brought agricultural revenue to a point where, divided among a diminishing number of persons, it released a surplus that then became available for the purchase of newly created industrial products. This admirable progress that brought fallow-land into cultivations, introduced forage crops and the production of selective strains of seeds, scientific crop rotation, and then, much later, Liebig's soil chemistry—all this progress was clearly part of the industrial phenomenon. They all proceed from the same mentality and from the same search that led to the improvement of spinning and weaving machines or the steam engine. If one goes further back in time one may see that as early as the thirteenth century Flanders had replaced the fallow land with catch-crops. Flanders was, along with northern Italy, one of the centres of capitalist activity during that period, as is indicated by its remarkable increase in population density. With the slowness and, above all, the high cost of transports, this population would have seen itself constantly threatened by famine had it not succeeded locally in increasing agricultural production in the way we have indicated. In consequence, there is no doubt that agriculture is a condition for capitalist economic activity. But equally it is a manifestation of it. Let us consider even more basic

[3] Or at least agricultural changes must precede it. For it took more than twenty years for those responsible for the economic destiny of the Third World to acknowledge that a flourishing industry could not be built up in the absence of an agricultural sector capable of producing significant surpluses. It must be hoped that it will not take so long for these same men to arrive at the conviction that neither agriculture nor industry will be obtained in the absence of a psychological transformation effected by the entrepreneurial spirit. Consequently, it clearly would seem that, to the extent that the non-industrialized countries intend to achieve stronger and more rapid economic growth, certain specific and straight-forward changes are required. It is necessary: first, to create or import entrepreneurs; second, to permit them to get about their business; third, to accept disruptions; fourth, to wait for twenty or thirty years. But it is so certain that economic growth is the primary objective of the leaders of non-industrial countries? Is it more important than national independence?

foundations of an economic system so as to get rid of a particularly tenacious illusion, that of technology. The first condition for increasing agricultural output was the employment of an implement capable of turning up the deep soil so as to bring to the surface and aerate nutritive substances. It was necessary for the heavy long-shared plough to replace the scratch-plough. Now, the introduction of the heavy plough probably dates back to the eighth or ninth century, which represents an era of widespread economic stagnation. In other words—and this point appears to me essential—a technical improvement may never be considered as the starting-point for economic progress: *there is a time-lag between the introduction of a technical operation and its general usage.* This discontinuity may grow into a paradox of history. Let us recall that the important discoveries of the windmill and the collared yoke (which, by transferring the strain to the animal's chest instead of its neck, permitted at the very least a quadrupling of the burden it could pull, from which came the possibility of increasing the efficiency of transports and, most importantly, of putting under cultivation the heavy clay soils of the great North European plain)—these discoveries probably date from the fifth century A.D., the same period that witnessed the economic and political disintegration of the Western Empire. They were not economically employed as a general policy in North-West Europe until the eleventh or twelfth centuries, when their use was tied to the prodigious advances of the capitalist system. We may take the quite different geographical and economic area of China for comparative evidence. In his monumental study,[4] Joseph Needham has shown that the technical competence of the Chinese was in no way inferior to that of Europeans; what was almost always absent was the intention of using their discoveries to obtain economic results. Thus, I tend to think that there exists a very wide range of autonomy between technical and economic activities (at least up to the present day). From the appearance of hominoid groups in the late paleolithic era, individuals, following their natural inclinations, have been devoted to technical pursuits and the improvement of procedures that may or may not have accommodated economic applications. Here one thinks of the vast amount of patience and ingenuity, the alternation, over thousands of years, of defeat and success that were necessary to perfect that technical masterpiece, the controlled flooding of the rice-paddies of monsoon Asia. In our own day, this empirical technical specialization

---

[4] *Science and Civilization in China* (Cambridge: Cambridge University Press, 1945–), 4 vols. to date (1971).

continues to exist, without direct or immediate ties to economic usage, in the *concours Lépine,* an annual event at which inventors present their work to the public and hope to find financial backing. The technical history of mankind may be considered as a gigantic *concours Lépine,* where geographical and temporal gaps between a discovery and its application can be enormous.

Thus, we may set forth our first methodological rule: everything that is understood as the conditions of an economic system is in fact part of it and thus cannot explain it. A second rule is: the specific psychological attitudes upon which an economic system rests are consequences of it and are not prior to it. In fact, whatever the kind of life considered, in order for individuals to move at their ease within the geographical, technical, economic, social, and religious framework where destiny has placed them, certain traits of their character and temperament must conform to the roles that society has waiting for them. Let us take an example.

M. Jean-Pierre Vernant has shown[5] what was the specifically Greek conception of the work of the artisan:

> Each craft constitutes ... a closed system within which everything is integrally organized around the perfection of the product to be made: the instruments, the technical operations, and, deep within the craftsman's very soul, certain specific qualities that belong only to him. ...
>
> A personal tie of dependence, a relationship of service, appears rather than is instituted between the maker and the user of a product. Within the field of his craft the capacities of the artisan are rigorously organized around his work, and his work is rigorously governed by the need of its user (p. 221).

To express these observations in a Marxian jargon, one would say that the use-value takes priority entirely over the exchange-value. Now, there is a logic to use-value: the object made has an inherent value as it serves a definite function; this value is determined by tradition or by a specific relationship with the world of ideas, and in any case, it is a datum that exists prior to the work. In the same way, the need that the

---

[5] *Mythe et pensée chez les Grecs: Études de psychologie historique* (Paris: Maspero, 1965).

object is called upon to satisfy is also a quasi-natural datum. It follows that the work of construction can only be very lowly, and is placed at the service of intangible needs and objects. But, on the other hand, when exchange-value is more important, all these relations are reversed: the object is no longer determinate and, from the moment it is considered worth acquiring, it can be anything at all; need is also unstable since there are no more subtle but necessary ties to bind it to imaginary objects. Such a situation necessarily places a high value upon labour as such, which is turned into a new demiurge, undifferentiated and placed above particular labourers who become but its humble servants. This brief analysis is intended to show that such a transformation of psychological relations to labour cannot have its origin in the mental conception itself. This is quite plain from the Greek example: such a psychological configuration is rigorously coherent, satisfactory for everyone concerned, and thus immutable. It can be altered only by the effect of basic alterations that are unexpected within the world of labour itself, or else by changes that take place at non-economic psychological levels. It follows that *in theory* every psychological alteration *may* have economic consequences. It would be necessary and sufficient for this modification to influence the system of needs or the relation of the worker to his work. Thus, it is appropriate to exclude from the definition of the phenomenon whose origins are sought every psychological datum that clearly would belong to the consequences of the phenomenon under investigation.

Now, then, what is the capitalist system? Analysis of Marx's theses has shown that it cannot be defined as the conjunction of capitalist ownership of the means of production with the wage-labourer who has neither hearth nor home. Not that this aspect is not a constituent element of the system (on the contrary, this is one of its original features), but because the investigation of origins that starts from such a statement obliges us to go round in circles. After all, those who would claim that the mode of appropriation of the means of production is essential are rare indeed today; generally one tends to argue by pointing to other oppositions, and in particular for those who make reference to the part played by power in economic activity, conflict is shifted to that between men invested with decision-making ability and those who execute their orders. However, at this point the definition becomes vague, for one can find such opposition in any economic system whatsoever, so much so that one may scarcely see how the particular characteristics of capitalism may appear at all. In pre-industrial agricultural systems the decision-making power of those who carry out orders is, so to speak, non-existent. A series of religious, magic, technical, and community restraints entirely subordinate the labourer to the will of the leader or the will of the gods. In the salt-works in China during the period of the T'ang, economic power belonged to the license-holder; in the workshops of Lysias' father in Athens it is hardly likely that the slaves had much to say about making shields. There is no difficulty in multiplying such examples from all civilizations and all stages of development: the unequal division of economic power is a constant. One could even maintain, without intending to be paradoxical or provocative—and I shall have to return to this matter—that the capitalist system is precisely the first economic organization that makes possible a more or less widespread participation of workers in decisions that concern them. As for what an economy without power, where each worker has an equal part in decisions, might possibly be, I shall wait to see it in operation before I will admit it is anything more than an intellectual's dream.

Shall we define capitalism in terms of a market-economy? This definition is no more specific than any other. In fact, the folly of Stalinist planning was necessary in order to show the impossibility of thinking that a modern economy that was not a market-economy could exist. Every economy, because it comes into being at the conjunction of producers and consumers, is a market-economy. But this conjunction is unstable: one of its limits is the strict determination by tradition of needs and ways of satisfying them, which reduces almost to nothing the problems of adjusting supply and demand. Its opposite limit is perfect competition, where a demand, free of all tradition and restraint is brought unimpeded into contact with a perfectly elastic supply. These are limiting cases. Historical reality is situated at various points on the scale between the two. It goes without saying that one must qualify severely these remarks about the market. Market and exchange cannot, strictly speaking, be equated. There is an exchange whenever any good changes hands. At this level of generalization, exchange exists in every society, even within a hypothetical original family, for goods would have been exchanged between husband and wife and among parents and children. A more limited form of exchange is represented by the *gift* and the *return gift* analysed by Marcel Mauss:[6]

[6] *The Gift: Forms and Functions of Exchange in Archaic Societies*, tr. Ian Cunnison (London: Cohen and West, 1966), pp. 1–16.

the exchange is governed by a whole series of rules that institutionalize and limit spontaneity. A third form of exchange would be the governmental regulatory tax whereby the surplus created by each element of an economic apparatus is entirely absorbed by the central power. The almost ideal type of governmental regulatory tax is found in pharaonic Egypt and even more in Ptolemaic Egypt: the surplus was confiscated by the central authority, which then proceeded to distribute it among the beneficiaries of the system. To tell the truth, under the Pharaohs, a part of the production of the fellahas and of the temples was dumped directly onto the market, without passing through the imperial storehouses. The same thing happened to the surplus that the mass of individual land-owners got rid of on the market in order to obtain clothing, furniture, and ornamental and luxury goods. These needs were met by the production of free artisans. And finally, there existed merchants in the strict sense, involved in all kinds of commercial business. Iconography as well as texts indicate, however, that this kind of trade involved relatively small quantities and the markets involved were purely local. Another form of trade could have been *reallotment*. The only known example seems to have been the Empire of the Incas where production was wholly monopolized by the central authorities and then distributed to all levels of society.

In the strict sense of the term, a market is an exchange that presupposes the autonomy of economic atoms trading with each other. It rests, therefore, upon the freedom of *do ut des*. In this sense, the market is a constant feature of all human societies, at least in the realm of economic relations among politically sovereign units. It is also prevalent in the most universal form of trade, wife-exchange. Whatever the degree of complexity, strictness, and precision of marriage rules, they never impose the marriage of a specific person upon another but always leave a margin of choice to the eventual husband and wife. In short, almost all known complex societies (outside of Peru) are a mixture of the market and governmental regulatory tax, which is accounted for by the fact that, prior to the industrial system, the greater part of production was consumed by the producers. Consequently, when I state that there is no economy in the absence of a market, it must be understood as being qualified according to the kind of society under consideration.

What this means for our definition is nothing less than the consideration that to define the capitalist system by the market is to neglect its historical specificity. Or, to be more precise, if it is true that Western capitalism pushed the extension of the market system to previously unknown limits, it is no less true that Mesopotamian, Greek, Hellenistic, Roman, Abbassid, and Chinese societies (to name only the most important) have also experienced a considerable development of the market. Consequently, to identify what is original about the West, it is necessary to introduce a quantitative criterion that may indicate a certain threshold of trade effected by the intermediary of the market beyond which the capitalist system may be found. It follows from this that one may not construct such a criterion. After all, from the eleventh to the seventeenth century the West revealed no substantial differences in this respect compared to other civilizations. Maurice Lombard[7] is probably right when he considers that Islam established an economic unity from lands that gradually over thousands of years had come to constitute the Mediterranean basin. This fusion brought with it a vast increase in trade that made the Abbassid world one of the most brilliant economic successes in history, even though it was short-lived. The West is not decisively distinguished by such examples until the eighteenth century. Now, as I intend to show below, the structural elements of capitalism were inscribed in the facts from as early as the eleventh century. Consequently, if the extent of the market in the capitalist system is an element that clearly must be taken into account, it is not sufficient to characterize it.

Capitalism can no longer be defined by profit-seeking since it is so widely distributed, at least, if the word profit is taken in the imprecise and general sense of obtaining supplementary utilities. One must have Rousseau's optimism concerning the goodness of human nature to consider that the profit-motive is tied to the appearance of private property and social life. Or else one must share his pessimistic view of social man in order to experience the need to invent the fiction of the goodness of natural man. Of course, it is difficult to decide what is right in this business of fundamentals. It seems to me to be more in accord with the facts and man's self-image to assume that desires are unlimited and that the spirit of covetousness belongs to man *qua* man. As covetousness is satisfied more easily by fraud than by honest labour, I tend to view the state of nature as did Hobbes and hold that, outside the social contract, *lupus est homo homini, non homo*. In order for any human group whatsoever simply to continue to exist, this spirit of covetousness must be limited and, in one way or another, internalized. It follows that the spirit of covetousness will be *internally* effective at

[7] *L'Islam dans sa première grandeur (VIII–XIe siècles)* (Paris: Flammarion, 1971).

the expense of other human groups. In other words, war is the first form taken by the profit-motive; and the most primitive objective of war that can be observed is the abduction of women since the possession of women is the scarce resource par excellence upon which the survival of the species depends.

Thus we must specify the capitalist mode of profit-seeking. Max Weber provides some pertinent guidelines.

> We will define a capitalist economic action as one which rests upon the expectation of profit by the utilization of opportunities for exchange, that is, on (formally) peaceful chances of profit. . . . Where capitalistic acquisition is rationally pursued, the corresponding action is adjusted to calculations in terms of capital. . . . Everything is done in terms of balances: at the beginning of the enterprise an initial balance, before every individual decision a calculation to ascertain its probable profitableness, and at the end a final balance to ascertain how much profit has been made. . . . For the purpose of this conception all that matters is that an actual adaptation of economic action to a comparison of money income with money expenses takes place, no matter how primitive the form (*Protestant Ethic*, pp. 17–19).

But that is not significant, for 'in this sense, capitalism and capitalistic enterprises, even with a considerable rationalization of capitalistic calculation, have existed in all civilized countries . . .' (p. 19). If we wish to produce an historical illustration of this statement of Max Weber's, we are faced with an embarrassment of riches. Thus, in ancient Mesopotamia there was the *Karum*. This word, of Akkadian origin, originally designated a river port and then, by extension, entrepots and commercial houses where importers, exporters, provisioners, and bankers all conducted their affairs. Occasionally these houses functioned as commercial tribunals. Paul Garelli[8] has been able to study the *Karum* in detail thanks to the recovery of several thousand Assyrian tablets, dating from the twentieth and nineteenth centuries B.C., at Cappadocia. They reveal a complete commercial network run by genuine capitalists. No doubt they were still closely tied to the State that contracted out certain taxes and tariffs and that supervised their activities by means of a pyramidal structure centred in Ashur.

[8] *Les Assyriens en Cappadoce* (Paris: Librarie Adrien Maisonneuve, 1963); cf. *Cambridge Ancient History*, 3rd ed., I: 2, pp. 721ff.

In spite of this state control, or at least state interference, the *Karum* had their own commercial activities and developed a series of institutions within which capitalist activity, as defined by Max Weber, took place. Banks undertook and granted loans; large warehouses brought together the merchandise of groups of merchants; bank accounts were opened where most of the operations were made by multilateral balancing of accounts. Sometime later, and certainly by the beginning of the second millennium, at Ur and then at Larsa, capitalism seemed to be entirely free of state control. Private entrepreneurs had replaced the temple and palace as disbursers of loans at interest (33 per cent *per annum*); they made advances to wholesale merchants and directed the copper imports. However, it was not until the neo-Babylonian and Achaemenid era (sixth to fourth century B.C.) that one may find banks whose activities have a more or less modern character. In Nippur and Babylon firms were created through the association of capitalists. They took in money deposits, issued cheques, made loans at interest, and, most importantly, participated directly in economic changes by investing in numerous agricultural and industrial enterprises.

There is another, more astonishing example given by Lombard[9] that is even closer to our own practices. From the eight to the eleventh century A.D. the Abbassid world was familiar with a fully developed capitalist activity. It was undertaken Muslim, Jewish, and Christian businessmen: once again we find an ancient and Eastern background to economic initiative. They created large commercial societies that pushed their tentacles in all directions where profits could be gathered: towards the Sudan, where salt and cheap goods were traded for gold, towards the Indian Ocean where the port of Basra received precious cargoes from as far away as China, towards the Russian rivers where slaves furnished the best chances for high profits. These large companies ended by establishing numerous branch offices all along their customary trade routes. In a parallel direction banks were created by pooling capital: these organizations carried on all the operations of a bank. And finally there appeared the decisive characteristic of capitalism, the merchant entrepreneur. This kind of person, who had grown wealthy by large-scale commerce, sought to increase his own capital in industrial enterprises, especially in textiles. He obtained the raw materials, entrusted it to workers to whom he provided financial advances, and then undertook to sell the finished product. The profits gained from all these activities were systematically reinvested. In short, the historian

[9] *L'Islam dans sa première grandeur*, pp. 149–50.

> But was there a free market in labor?

discovers a feverish and dynamic business world that stands second to none in the medieval and modern West.

Thus I could take one civilization after another and everywhere (or nearly everywhere, for there are symptomatic exceptions to which I shall have to revert) I would find capitalists whose activity 'rests on the expectation of profit by the utilization of opportunities for exchange'. There is no mystery involved: the starting point of its evolution and its internal logic appears to me—very generally—to be as follows:

In the beginning was the creation of empires, by which is to be understood every political system encompassing a geographical area and a population of such a size that a State bureaucracy, even if only embryonic, is necessary. The forms taken by this creation are ever hidden by gaps in the documentary evidence for the simple reason that written documents would only appear after something like a bureaucracy was needed to create archival records and set up a responsible administration, to publish laws and transmit orders. Without trusting overmuch the imagination of the historian, it is legitimate to suppose that this was only possible through conquest or progressive expansion outward from a heartland: war must have been the great midwife of civilizations. Such activity led to the decisive appearance of a political, military, and religious elite characterized by being exempt from providing itself with its subsistence needs. It follows that the system of subsistence production had to have achieved a degree of efficiency such that once the amount needed for the maintenance of the producers and their families was deducted, along with the obligatory reserves needed for seeds, there still remained a surplus that this elite could confiscate. It was in this situation that, so far as I can tell, there are reasons to suspect a fundamental change, dating from the neolithic era, namely the adoption of agricultural and stockbreeding techniques by human groups. Not that the *invention* of these two technologies was itself necessarily attributable to matters that, in the final analysis, were political; as I have already suggested, technical invention is probably a free activity coeval with *homo faber*, who appeared in the later paleolithic era. In this sense it matters not where agriculture and the domestication of certain animals could have been invented nor whether it happened simultaneously or successively in different times and places. On the other hand, the systematic *extension* of new technologies and their economical employment are tied to the existence of empires and the appearance of an imperial elite.

The link is apparent in the example of so-called hydraulic agrarian systems where agricultural production is based upon drainage works or soil irrigation or, as most frequently happens, the two together. Karl Wittfogel's Marxist-inspired thesis[10] is well-known: despotic states and bureaucracies are established in order to ensure that maintenance and repair work, indispensable for agricultural production, are maintained. An inverse thesis seems to me to conform to the facts better: it is because a centralized political power has been created by war that maintenance and repair work could be conducted properly. Demonstration of this is fairly easy. Disorganization of the Egyptian irrigation system regularly *followed* the decline of political power, a decline determined by struggles within the elite. In the same way Ifriqiya (the ancient Roman province of Africa and the future Tunisia and part of Algeria) ceased to be a wheat- and oil-producing area, as it had been for thousands of years, in the wake of the destruction caused by the Hilali invasion during the tenth century.[11] Ceylon provides even more surprising evidence. In our own time population and activity has been concentrated in the mountains of the South while the Centre and North have been abandoned to jungle, swamps, and malaria. But from the fifth century B.C. to the thirteenth century A.D. the centre of Singhalese civilization was established precisely in these now uninhabited areas. Thanks to a State capable of undertaking large-scale irrigation (12,000 dammed reservoirs fed a whole canal system and were themselves fed by rivers and streams flowing from the central highlands) a brilliant society could be built. Decline began about the twelfth century and the sequence of events was characteristic: the monarchy declined, there was civil unrest, the invasion of the Tamils, anarchy. The system of dams and canals fell into disrepair, famines multiplied, population declined and sought refuge in the mountains of the South, leaving their former homeland to scrub forests, stagnant water, and mosquitos.

On this point, as on the others, there is no lack of historical examples to support the thesis that the ultimate basis of economic activity must be sought in the realm of politics. If I have insisted upon the primary role of state power to explain the fundamental changes of the neolithic era, even at the risk of the impression of losing the thread of my argument, it is precisely because, as will appear below, I consider that the key to the problem of the origins of capitalism is found on the side of the political system.

[10] *Oriental Despotism* (New Haven: Yale University Press, 1957).
[11] For a brief account see *The Cambridge History of Islam*, II, pp. 220ff.

But, to return to our merchants: the appearance of an elite living on a confiscated surplus *ipso facto* creates a market, which is to say, a financially solvent source of demand. The merchant is the indispensable intermediary for exchanges that satisfy this demand. It goes without saying that the actual material involved in these exchanges varies with the state of civilization and is diversified according to the degree of technical achievement in the domain of armaments, clothing, furniture, plates and dishes, jewellery, and so forth. At the same time, long-distance commerce appears, brought about by the demand for specific primary materials: gold, silver, tin, and copper. From this derives a secondary market that business-men may profit by. And finally, the extension of the State and its system of finances opens the way to a third type of capitalist activity: contracting for public revenues. This third source of capitalism depends inversely upon the degree of perfection achieved by the state apparatus. Generally the development of certain areas of production, which are subject to state monopoly, is contracted out to specialized entrepreneurs, for these enterprises have extensive manpower demands and require specialized equipment. This is the case with salt deposits, owing to the fact that salt is physiologically indispensable and easily monopolized since it is found in only a few places and demands a relatively large investment in equipment. For this reason state monopoly of salt is a universally prevalent means of raising revenue.

These brief remarks bring me to a decisive conclusion: The degree of capitalist activity achieved in any given society is defined by the intersection of two curves. The one is determined by the area governed by the society, by the number of people in the society, and by the amount of wealth created by a given state of technology. The other is determined by the degree of autonomy that the state grants to trading activities. The more that the State undertakes to arrogate the surplus to itself and to redistribute it as well, the less will any capitalist activity be able to take place. In the extreme it will disappear altogether. The Empire of the Incas provides us with a perfect example. As we noted above, it was characterized by a total State control over all social and especially economic activities. The redistribution of revenue was entirely run by the central power. The result was a total absence of merchants and capitalist activities. Only in recently conquered provinces and on the periphery of the empire did commerce remain flourishing; to the extent that as the provinces were incorporated into the imperial system, commerce declined and eventually disappeared. The only merchants who continued to exist were those who were responsible for importing those products that were not found in the Andean uplands. Upon occasion the Incas were not above using such men as spies.

If it be conceded that the state of technology has until very recently changed but slowly, and that variations in the level of population have depended directly upon the dangers involved in domestic and foreign policy (even while admitting that its maximum was determined by available sustenance and agricultural technique) the conclusion imposes itself that the two curves are influence by politics. Thus I revert to the same proposition: when all is said and done, the solution to the problem of the origins of capitalism must be sought within the political system.

Thus, it is not sufficient to characterize capitalism by the employment of peaceful opportunities for profit: a supplementary determinative factor must be introduced. Max Weber had recourse to the following: 'in modern times the Occident has developed . . . a very different form of capitalism which has appeared nowhere else: the rational capitalistic organization of (formally) free labour' (*Protestant Ethic*, p. 21). The essential and fundamental trait is the rational organization of labour. Thus what is involved is an explanation of 'the origin of this sober bourgeois capitalism with its rational organization of free labour' (*Protestant Ethic*, p. 24). If we leave aside for a moment the qualification of 'free' labour (to which we shall revert below), the defining feature of capitalism is, thus, according to Max Weber, the rational organization of labour. I have not been convinced that this definition, as finally adopted by him, would be useful in my research. What I need is a characteristic feature of the western economic system that is found nowhere else, not simply in terms of quantitative differences or differences of degree, but absolutely. Now, the rational organization of labour, even if one adds the qualification 'free' has nothing specifically Western about it: it may be found in one form or another in every human society. In fact, one could even say that an economy exists from the moment when a human need is satisfied by a labour. This could be expressed in yet another way: the economy exists in virtue of the fact that goods are scarce and must be raised to the level of needs.[12] Every

[12] This is why a society lacking all economic activities is inconceivable unless we fall victim to utopian dreams of a golden age or an earthly paradise, that is to say, to the dream of worlds of abundance.

economic act contains a core of rationality since it is based upon a search for maximum effectiveness and minimum cost. Whatever the type of economy considered this rule holds good, if only because man is naturally lazy. One can scarcely conceive of ordinary average men regularly expending greater physical and mental efforts than required to obtain the goods required to satisfy their needs. The general conditions for economic efficiency are easily defined. They imply:

1. *The division of labour and its necessary corollary, exchange.* The importance of the division of labour is plain: the greater the number of distinct tasks a society has to complete and of processes whose accomplishment is predicated upon a clearly independent status, the more efficient will human action be, for society would then be able to have such and such a group specialize in such and such a task. By eliminating waste time and useless motions, and by perfecting new and more efficient procedures, a specialist will be able better to reduce the time necessary to finish a task. The division of labour is observed in every society, even the most archaic, if only in terms of a partition of tasks according to sex and age. It makes little difference whether we know this original division has a religious or a biological basis: the fact is that it always exists.

The division of labour is necessarily accompanied by exchange since a whole range of specific products is required to satisfy the needs of a social group. Consequently, as was stated, every society is familiar with a minimum of exchange. Reciprocally, exchange brings to light the intrinsic rationality of the division of labour. If one man is particularly good at making loin-cloths and another at making masks, it would be in their interest to specialize, each within his own sector, and then exchange their products. It follows, however, that they could only obtain this experience and advantage if they had in fact undertaken exchanges and were able to make comparisons. In other words, for the advantages of a division of labour to be evident, a given society must have already developed a certain level of trade and exchange. Consequently, in the course of history, some exchanges are motors for change. This consideration leads me to formulate the following crucial propositions: *the more that exchanges are intensified within a society, the greater the division of labour and the more efficient this society will be.* This may be expressed in another way: *the more that use-value is replaced by exchange-value, the more efficient the society: the most efficient being that society where everything has a price and may be exchanged without impediment.* In fact this would be a theoretical limit that even our own present-day societies have not attained.

It may not be out of place here to recall Ricardo's law of comparative advantage, which shows that exchange is not only advantageous when those who make the exchange each excel in one field but also when one of the two surpasses the other in *two* fields. Ricardo argued in terms of an exchange of textiles and wines between England and Portugal[13] but we shall take our former example: if the first individual is better at making both loin-cloths and masks, the search for maximum efficiency demands that the first specializes in whatever brings him the most *comparative* advantage over the second and the second in whatever makes him *comparatively* least worst off. The whole system will be the most efficient one possible, for each producer will be specialized in what he is relatively the most suited for. As the number of parties to the exchange and the number of products increases, things get more complicated, but the law remains fundamentally valid. According to Paul Samuelson, if a beauty contest for the laws of economics were held, the law of comparative advantage would win first prize.

2. *The use of money* in its triple function as an instrument of measuring value, as a medium of exchange, and as a reserve for purchasing power. This follows directly from the first point. Exchange is an economic necessity, but no exchange is possible without reference to a universal equivalent, at least in the abstract. Thus, in pharaonic Egypt there was no money in the sense that we understand the term and all exchanges were made on the basis of a system of barter. Wages, even those of the highest officials, were paid out in natural products. For example, at the beginning of the Eighteenth Dynasty (in the early sixteenth century B.C.) the second prophet of Amon received a salary of gold, silver, and copper articles, clothing, head-veils, perfume, servants, wheat, and lands. But these barter-exchanges were not haphazard: they were made with reference to a theoretical metallic standard (copper, silver, or gold, according to the importance of the transactions) and each good had a specific price despite the absence of any real money. The same was true in Mesopotamia: there was no money but there were different standards represented by cereals and especially by metals. In China during the T'ang period, copper coinage was too inconvenient for transactions involving large sums. In order to undertake such transactions the Chinese used not a theoretical standard as in Egypt and Mesopotamia
[13] Cf. *Principles of Political Economy*, Ch. VII.

but a concrete one, namely silk (in the form of clothing), and precious metals (generally silver). These two forms of money were used equally for public and private exchange.[14]

These three examples serve to show that if *money* appears everywhere and always, there is not everywhere and always *currency*. The distinction between these two notions is made more easily in German. On the one side there is *die Münze* (which I translate as *currency*): it is used to designate every sign (whether metallic, paper, leather, etc.) backed by a political power and serving as a medium of exchange, a standard of value, and a reserve for purchasing power. On the other side is *das Geld* (which is rendered as *money*): it refers to everything invested with these functions, whether tacitly or explicitly. If money-*Geld* is universal, currency-*Münze* was born in the world of Greek antiquity. The beauty of the whole thing is that the introduction of currency was not undertaken for economic reasons but for religious and especially political ones. Edouard Will, taking up and developing the hypotheses of B. Laum[15] and his pupils[16] has come up with a theory[17] that I should summarize as follows.

On the basis of an analysis of the Homeric poems, Laum concluded that the appraisal of goods came from sacrifices and the determination of an offering: money-*Geld* first served as the means of payment between mortals and immortals. As the foundation of money, one must take account of the notions of rewards and release from debt. Subsequently these notions were laicised and related to the idea of compensatory social justice For example, according to Aristotle (*Eth. Nic.* 1132b 32ff.) money 'serves to maintain the reciprocity of social relations on the level of justice'.[18] This ethical and social side of money, is confirmed by the semantics of the Greek root 'nem-' as in νόμος, νομίζω, νόμισμα, νέμω, νέμεσις and so forth, that indicate a series of moral qualifications indicating estimation, reciprocity, moral worth,

[14] D. C. Twitchett, *Financial Administration under the T"ang Dynasty*, 2nd ed. (Cambridge: Cambridge University Press, 1970), pp. 70ff.

[15] *Heiliges Geld: Eine historische Untersuchung über den sakralen Ursprung des Geldes* (1924), and *Über das Wesen des Münzgeldes* (1929).

[16] Especially W. Gerloff, *Die Entstehung des Geldes und die Anfänge des Geldwesens*, 3rd ed. (1947).

[17] Edouard Will, 'De l'aspect éthique des origines grecques de la monnaie', *Revue historique*, 212 (1954), pp. 209–21; *idem.*, 'Reflexions et hypothèses sur les origines du monnayage' *Revue numismatique*, 17 (1955), pp. 5–23; *idem.*, *Korinthiaka* (Paris: De Boccard, 1955), pp. 495–502.

[18] Will, 'De l'aspect éthique . . .', p. 218.

equality, harmony, etc., and opposed to ὕβρις, which implies an absence of order and an outburst of force.[19]

The politico-social etiology of currency-*Münze* is confirmed by the example of Corinth. The first issue of currency dates from the closing years of the seventh century B.C. under the tyranny of Cypselus. Will recounts the events in the following way: Cypselus began by confiscating the lands of one of the large families, the Bacchiadae, and redistributed them. That took care of the problem of their land but not of their debts, the second great problem of ancient Greece. In order to deal with this problem, he had to mint the articles of silver confiscated from the Bacchiadae into coins and distribute them to the people; thus he redeemed their debts toward the nobility whom he had not despoiled. In order to prevent an instantaneous restoration of inequalities and to stimulate the circulation of currency, Cypselus had to impose a second measure, a tax of 10 per cent for ten years on the income of Corinthians. Public expenses, financed by this direct tax, came to be used to initiate and maintain the circulation of currency.

This clever but purely theoretical reconstruction of Will is entirely confirmed by the wholly independent research of C. M. Kraay.[20] The author wished to verify a double hypothesis on the basis of his study of ancient Greek coin-hoards. If the function of currency is first of all commercial, the finds of coin-hoards will be well dispersed along the routes of international commerce. Nothing of the kind has been discovered: currency is only very slightly dispersed: Italian coins are generally found in Italy, Sicilian ones in Sicily, and Corinthian coins in Corinth. In Athens there was practically no export of coins until the last quarter of the sixth century. Under the same hypothesis, one would expect a division of money into fractions for purposes of local commerce. Now this development was very slow throughout the whole Greek world. On the whole, the essentially local areas served by the circulation of currency do not coincide with those of commerce. Consequently, the currency function is not primarily one of exchange. This confirms the alternative hypothesis that the minting of coins was tied to the needs of the State: payment of mercenaries, public works, fines, regulation of social problems. A final bit of evidence may be added: minting of coins appeared in Egypt a little before Alexander's

[19] According to E. Laroche 'Histoire de la racine "nem-" en grec ancien', *Études et commentaires* VI (1949).

[20] 'Hoards, Small Change and the Origin of Coinage', *Journal of Hellenic Studies*, 84 (1964), pp. 76–91.

conquest when the Nilotic pharaohs were fighting against Persian occupation and recruited Greek mercenaries for the job.

It goes without saying that, once begun, minting of coins considerably facilitated economic exchanges and that in turn the extension of trade encouraged further minting. Thus it is perfectly normal for the economic use of money to increase quite rapidly.

3. *The improvement of book-keeping* permitted losses and gains, costs and profits and, above all, credits and debits to be kept. Of course, book-keeping, at least in embryo, must exist everywhere, if only to arrive at an equilibrium of exchange. In every society the algebraic sum of exchanges must always be equal to zero; if not, the system would rapidly decline and end up being paralysed. Even in a society like the Egyptian, where government requisition and distribution became the dominant system, goods were referred to a basic standard as a form of protection against external aggression or internal anarchy, of intercession to obtain the blessing of the gods and of aid in the event of a natural disaster. If this were not done, order would deteriorate, the people would rebel or go on strike (as, for example in the ἀναχώρησις during the Ptolemaic era); in short, the social contract was broken. Likewise, in every agrarian society there must be at least an account record that fixes the amount to be divided between the consumable harvest and the seed needed for subsequent planting.

When a group attains the social form of Empire, as it has been defined above, keeping of accounts becomes indispensable. In fact, the production of a balance-sheet is divided up among different beneficiaries: the State, the bureaucrats, property-owners, temples, monasteries and, of course, the producers themselves. In order to ensure a correct distribution, accounts must be kept. They are even more necessary for those on the receiving end. The sovereign (the Pharaoh, for example, or the Inca) concentrates the product connected by regulatory taxes in central and local stores where it is then re-divided for the maintenance of the sovereign and his entourage, the bureaucrats, the army and so on. All these movements of goods must be registered in an account-book divided into credits and debits. The most likely hypothesis, as I suggested above, is that writing developed from the need to keep such accounts. As evidence we may note that the main feature of the hundreds of thousands of cuneiform tablets discovered in Mesopotamia have preserved the accounts of palace clerks, just as the recent (1953) decyphering of Linear-B revealed the secrets of the tablets of Cnossos,

Plyos, and Tiryns and showed them to comprise for the most part the King's book-keeping archive. Personally, I would be willing to consider the Inca *quipu* as a first rough attempt at a system of writing, one that never had time to develop fully. The *quipu* was a rope to which smaller strings of various colours were attached, some in parallel and some at angles to each other. The *quipu* designated both numbers and objects or ideas, with knots indicating the former and colours the latter. A whole series of complications and conventions made the *quipu* an efficient technique for memorizing concrete data. Now, this system may be used for keeping accounts: its purpose was to keep a record of all credits and debits of the social system (and not just the economic system, for demographic data were included in it). The whole thing served as an authoritative statistical service for the whole hierarchy, right down to the lowest administrative echelon.

Another social institution is particularly propitious for the development of book-keeping because it is indispensable for it: temples and monasteries. Whether as a result of individual donations or those of an established political power, they find themselves disposing of considerable revenues that must be exactly known and accounted for before they are redistributed for the daily needs of the community, for cultural buildings, for charitable works, for capital investments (such as land clearance and improving sanitation) and finally, for redistributions that Max Weber identified by the untranslatable term *Verpfründung* (which involves a system whereby the revenues of the temple or monastery are assigned to such and such a beneficiary who is designated by the monastic community or by the State). All of these activities clearly rest upon a more or less complex labour of book-keeping.

4. *The rational ordering of means*, whether intellectual, muscular, or technical, where rational is understood to mean the appropriate use of a means with respect to the end pursued. In this sense magic is a rational means since its use can be considered appropriate within a given society. Of course, this does not prejudge the efficacy of a rational use and everyone will admit that manure and fertilizer are more effective than the blessing of fields.

Modern men have an unfortunate tendency to be of the opinion that pre-modern techniques are simple and easily mastered. Nothing of the kind is true. Chipping flint properly demands a lengthy apprenticeship and even making a fire by rubbing two sticks together is not an immediate datum of human knowledge. Theodora Kroeber has told how American anthropologists have had to spend long hours learning from Ishi the proper technique of making fire.[21] In the same way, agricultural techniques (such as seed and soil selection, preparation of fields, improved sowing techniques, protection against animal and vegetable parasites) are admirable improvements, which have been obtained only after thousands of tentative gropings, some efforts being successful and others not. Now, the progressive selection of the most efficient and effective solutions is an eminently rational activity.

It is necessary to insist strongly that these four conditions are all equally connected to economic efficiency. This amounts to saying that in every human society, whatever it may be, efficiency is found at least in embryonic form because every society rests ultimately upon an economic basis and therefore is endowed with a certain degree of efficiency. If not, it disappears, purely and simply. Inversely, what results from this consideration is that in every investigation of the origin of an economic system it is vain to hope to find it in any one of these conditions. Modifications of them are always the consequences of changes that have chanced to arrive from somewhere else.

Thus, the invention of double-entry book-keeping is not the cause of medieval economic development, nor was the bill of exchange (they appeared at the dawn of the lengthy depression of the fourteenth and fifteenth centuries), but the adaptations of book-keeping and currency took place at the same times as the vast increase in trade from the eleventh to the thirteenth centuries. In any case, the invention of the bill of exchange is no mark of Western originality. Roman conquests during the first and second century turned Rome into a great financial centre. Capital from all over the Mediterranean flowed to it; it was a centre of large-scale financial speculation; loans were negotiated there and participation in financial or commercial enterprises was arranged. Great commercial banks were a part of the social landscape. And the bill of exchange was extensively used. Likewise in China[22] from about

---

[21] Theodora Kroeber, *Ishi in Two Worlds: A Biography of the Last Wild Indian in North America* (Berkeley and Los Angeles: University of California Press, 1961), Ch. 9. Gaston Bachelard, in his *The Psychoanalysis of Fire*, tr. A. C. M. Ross (London: Routledge & Kegan Paul, 1964), Ch. 4, has noted that the highly elaborate characteristics of this technology may be understood in terms of a transposition of sexual intercourse.

[22] Twitchett, *Financial Administration*, p. 72.

A.D. 750 on, a widespread use of the bill of exchange has been found (with the imaginative name, flying money, *fei-ch'ien*). The use of such bills served to transfer considerable sums of money in connection with the development of the tea business in the south of the country. Consignments of tea were compensated by payments that the government, which was situated in the north, raised through taxes in its southern provinces. There was no mystery involved here and certainly no need to appeal to the notion of borrowing or diffusion of techniques. Essentially all a bill of exchange amounts to is a means of making payment orders circulate instead of metallic currency tokens. As payments reached a level where the material transport of currency tokens was a problem, it would be normal enough that orders would be substituted for them. By this means the awkwardness of transport and risk of loss along the route were both removed. Naturally, for the bill of exchange to become a common device, payments between different areas had to be in equilibrium: everything was governed by adjustments and sets of documents, and only the balance, whether positive or negative, was the occasion for a transfer of funds. Incidentally, this condition of equilibrium between different parts of the empire suggests that at Rome, because of the centralized structure of the financial system where everything converged upon Rome, the use of bills of exchange must have remained limited. At a later day, the development of an equilibrium between the two principal centres of activity, northern Italy and Flanders, allowed the bill of exchange to become part of their daily life and to follow the development of trade from these two areas.

All this appears to me to be clear enough. What is less so is the parallel assertion that an extension of trade can never be considered as the cause for a basic alteration in economic activity. The level of trade is fixed for each economic system, and is bound to it by unbreakable ties. An important proposition follows from this, which we will use again below: the growth of trade through the extension of the market, whether by a simple spatial extension or by an increased conversion of use-values into exchange-values, does not owe its origin to economic activities themselves, but must be explained by changes that have occurred in another sphere of social activities. Expressed in another way, this proposition amounts to saying that a fundamental change in an economic system can only come from the outside.

Five: *The Essence of Capitalism*

By nature therefore, every economic act is rational, and aims at maximum efficiency. Economic efficiency, however, is limited (with a good deal of variation) by the interference of other values—religious, magic, ethical, political and so on. Now, the most original feature of Western capitalism, which distinguishes it radically from all other economic systems, is its real efficiency. It is the first system that may be characterized by a massive and, up to now, limitless increase in production, circulation, and consumption. The question that I have to deal with thus may be posed in the following terms: why has the West, and it alone, known an economic system characterized by the real maximisation of efficiency? Or again, why may the economic behaviour of Western men, and of them alone, be characterized by the incessant quest for maximum efficiency? These two propositions are not equivalent: the first suggests that an economic system is developed by itself in virtue of its own internal logic; the second puts the accent on the activity of men who make the system go. They need not do so in complete awareness of what is happening but only as a result of a host of local actions whose algebraic sum constitutes the system. A system is not an historical object but an *a posteriori* intellectual construction. Consequently, to start from the system in order to explain the genesis of it is impossible, as I have shown with the example of Marx. Not that I consider this procedure to be illegitimate: on the contrary, it is acceptable, but only on condition of taking the phenomenon once it has become fully developed in order to reconstruct it ideally by developing certain aspects and neglecting others. When one is interested in origins such a procedure is impossible. One must start off with the real behaviour of subjects and try to explain them.

Why, then, did western behaviour turn towards a search for maximum economic efficiency? Put this way the problem is insoluble.

In order to grasp this essential point let us consider a simple example, the birth-rate. Under the hypothesis of complete freedom of union between sexes and perfect indifference as to the consequences of this union, the birth-rate would attain its biological maximum, which has been estimated at around 70 per thousand. Whenever this 'natural' rate is not attained it means that obstacles have been imposed upon sexual union or the attitude toward conception is restrictive. The result is that each time the birthrate rises the increase must be imputed to the lifting of some kind of restraint. Consequently, every question concerning the increase in the birthrate must always be posed negatively: what has a given population done to give up limiting its fecundity? To complete the argument it is appropriate to add this: the natural rate is what it is only within the framework of a biological constitution that is given for man. A natural or deliberate alteration of this constitution (for example, a shortening of pregnancies or a systematic multiplication of plural births) would modify the framework and, consequently, the order of size of the birthrate.

If I were to generalize this example, I would obtain a proposition that may be stated thus: *there is a definite condition of human activities within any specific order (economics, politics, ethics, aesthetics, and so on) where these activities develop according to their own law and where, consequently, these activities attain their natural limits.* Activity always tends toward this limit, which is to say that it admits of no intrinsic stopping point.

This proposition seems to me to be sufficiently important to merit further elaboration.

It is Clausewitz's immortal achievement to have clarified what he called the concept of *war*, that is to say, its internal logic. War is a duel by which we intend to impose our will upon an adversary through the use of violence. This imposition becomes possible from the moment when the adversary is disarmed, so the disarming of the enemy becomes the goal of the operations of war. It follows from the nature of war that it tends necessarily towards extremes and thus becomes a struggle to the death. And this occurs because of three dialectically related movements called by him, reciprocal actions. In the first place, there is no intrinsic limitation to the manifestation of violence, for he who is unsparing in his use of violence has an advantage over him who uses restraint. In the second place, disarmament is the goal of both adversaries, so that each must try and beat his enemy under pain of being beaten. In the third place, the efforts of each one, in order to be victorious, must exceed the will and the capabilities of the other. As each one makes the same calculation there is no limit to their commitment.

Now, experience shows that war is only exceptionally a struggle to the death. Thus, certain limitations must have become established to limit the escalation to extremes. There are three. First, the two adversaries have some degree of knowledge of each other and can calculate the capability and the will of the other. They regulate their efforts in proportion to this calculation which serves, therefore, as a principle of moderation. Next, in the event, the first engagement is not decisive. Thus, war is undertaken over the long term, and each adversary will proportion his efforts to what he estimates to have to be those of the other. Finally, defeat is always a relative thing and may in the future be redeemed. The hope of a future reversal inspires moderation in the commitment of forces.

Even if Clausewitz did not expressly say so, invariably these restraints play a subordinate role compared to the escalation to extremes. It follows that every change in the effectiveness of these restraints will have as an immediate consequence the accentuation of the characteristic of a struggle to the death. If, for example, the parties to the conflict are completely unknown to each other (this is the case with conflicts between societies belonging to areas of wholly independent cultures such as that between Europeans and the native inhabitants of the New World), the war will have a tendency to be a war of extermination. It will be the same if the belligerents refuse to recognize each other, for then they would be living in two ideologically different worlds. This is the case in wars of religion or with the Nazi-Soviet conflict. If enemies cannot count upon the long-term results, or if mutual defeat is irremediable, escalation to extremes will necessarily occur. This would be so under the hypothesis of a nuclear war between the United States and the Soviet Union.

I have tried to make a similar analysis of revolutionary phenomena.[23] Because of the arbitrariness of values, and because the institutions and inequalities that result from the division of goods, such as wealth,

[23] *Les Phénomènes révolutionnaires* (Paris: P.U.F., 1970). English translation, *Revolution*, Oxford, Blackwell and New York, Harper & Row, 1975.

prestige and power, that are by nature rare, every society tends towards self-destruction. It seems to me that every society is familiar with conflicts that feed these three sources. Moreoever, if no limit is imposed upon them, they drive a society to dissolution in anarchy and eventually it perishes. Now, here as well, experience shows that this kind of development is quite exceptional. Thus, restraints are involved here too. The strongest and most constant is the fact that in a situation where forces of order directly face those of revolution, order normally benefits from a decisive superiority both in terms of numbers and capabilities and in terms of will. There is, of course, a genuine struggle to the death, but its frequency is limited by the small number of combatants. A second restraint results from the fact that every society develops mechanisms of socialization by which rules and norms assure order, and which are imposed upon new members of society, namely the young. As a result, most members of society grow up in such a way that they become used to, and satisfied by, the lot that falls to them. Or at least they contain their discontent within limits compatible with the maintenance of order. These restraints are secondary compared to the logic of disintegration, which means that every change in the restraint-mechanism will tend to increase revolutionary tensions. If order does not use, or uses badly, the force it monopolizes, the revolution will triumph. Now, theory and experience proves that the most general condition for such a contingency to transpire is division within the ruling elite. If the mechanisms of socialization seize up, revolutionary demonstrations will, by the same token, multiply: the most probable occasion for such a situation is uncertainty, not with respect to the mechanisms, but to the rules and norms to be imposed. I trust the reader will forgive this highly simplified summary. It is important mainly as an indication of the orders of priority within a system designed to explain complex phenomena.

A second example is *political power*. All power essentially consists in the possibility of a man or a group to influence the behaviour of others according to their own will. In this sense, all power tends towards absolute power, for the imposition of one will knows no other natural limit than the annihilation of the will of others. This is achieved when the annihilated will welcomes with joy and gratitude the violence that is done to it. The prince reaches supreme power when his subjects give their lives enthusiastically for a secret cause that he alone knows, which means that the value of sacrifice belongs entirely to the sacrifice itself. Even if such a situation is not wholly unknown in history (it may be found, for example, in religious contexts where the believer joyfully is obliterated before divine power), it is, nevertheless, rare. Once more, restraints are at work.

To proceed upon a complete account would take us beyond the scope of this essay, and we must rest content with a few indications of the road to be taken. First of all are obstacles of a material order. Numbers and space serve as limits to the exercise of the prince's will so that he must be content with a simply negative submission: it is enough for him that his subjects do not act dissidently. In the same way, technical necessities constrain him to consent to delegating power. And for good reason: he cannot personally supervise everything. It follows that the prince is necessarily motivated by a thirst for absolute power. It is possible, and even probable, that there exist in every society individuals who entertain such desires and ambitions, although the chance that they actually will attain power is slight. In fact, the prince is selected by mechanisms that tend to eliminate or neutralize these kinds of personalities. In the end, the plurality and competition of interests and convictions make it difficult for him simultaneously to impose an unlimited will equally in the areas of religion, the army, the administration, and so on. Generally, he will have to rely upon one instrument against the others, which confers a certain degree of autonomy on the first as well as on the others.

These restraints—and there are others—may lose their effectiveness. The improvement of the technical processes of collection and transmission of information considerably enlarges the possibilities of overcoming these obstacles of numbers and space. The means available to any contemporary leader are of an entirely different order than those available to princes in the pre-technical era. When the seat of power is vacant and open to the competition of ambitions drawn from all over the horizon and from all levels of society, the probability is increased that a man thirsty for absolute power will be able to prevail. This is why examples of tyranny are connected to profound social crises and revolutionary events. When the prince is driven by a revolutionary ideology and when large numbers of people share it, the obstacle of divergent opinions will have been removed, and his power will tend more easily to become absolute. The danger will be so much the greater when the ideology is defined by the actual holder of power rather than an independent authority, as would be the case with revealed religion. I could extend these remarks: but all of them would tend to indicate that the possibility, if not the probability, of a power

E

becoming absolute has been considerably enhanced by developments of contemporary civilization.

I have the weakness of thinking that these reflections have some importance. Human societies are constantly threatened by changes that would push them into extreme situations which, in turn, would simultaneously mean their death. Only by a series of restraints, whether by making some things, which will vary according to the technical level of society, impossible or by re-equilibrating forces that arise from life in society—whatever they are, only such restraints have, generally speaking, avoided catastrophes. Nothing allows us to affirm that this good luck has been forever guaranteed to humanity. With this in mind, I return to a consideration of capitalism from which, only superficially, have I departed. Capitalism is the state the economy must attain when nothing arises to hinder its law, that is, the law of efficiency.

The model of a society where efficiency would be maximized may be constructed. It presupposes:

1. That *the producers* have as their sole objective the search for maximum profits, not at all in order to enjoy the goods of this world, but simply for profit itself. This passion must, therefore, be accompanied by a rigorous asceticism that pushes savings to the limit permitted by the necessities of survival. Savings must then be systematically re-invested. Every superfluous expenditure, every playful activity, must be prohibited. Such a picture provides a caricature of the capitalist entrepreneur. But it is one that scarcely distorts reality. The Protestant ethic is not at all indispensable—even if it does allow us to understand certain particular features—for an explanation of the behaviour of capitalist entrepreneurs in any society whatsoever. They are all more or less approximated by this caricature: profit-seeking for no other reason than to obtain profits, and the systematic multiplication of opportunities for profit. Capitalists in all times and in all places seem to have a family resemblance. This may be explained by the fact that, where capitalist activities exist, they produce a type of man particularly adapted to such conditions. Personally, I would rather tend to think that in every society there exist individuals who have an excessive desire to possess and to take risks, for these two passions coexist within the capitalist spirit. However unfavourable the circumstances, such men can assert themselves and display their cleverness. What inclines me to this interpretation is—apart from my conviction about the unity of

human nature and the limited number of modes by which human destinies may be fulfilled—the fact that, as in the examples I have already produced and in others that I shall produce below, they clearly suggest that each time reality is suitable for him, the capitalist is there. Nothing suggests that his appearance necessitates a basic change in mentality: quite simply, he is there, entirely formed and adapted to his task. My interpretation in terms of the permanence of human types appears to me to be the most economical explanation of this fact.

2. That the *intellectual activity* of the society be entirely devoted to the creation of scientific and technical procedures that permit the lowering of costs. All free research undertaken simply for the satisfaction of understanding must be banned. Granted, it is not easy to make a distinction between pure or gratuitous research and research that is not. A research enterprise undertaken for purely speculative reasons may receive industrial applications that were entirely unintended. I do not insist upon this problem, which has become a common ground for political and journalistic arguments. Let us say rather that intellectual activity must be ordered so as to lead everywhere to practical applications of research.

3. That the *labourers* (and everyone must have a job, which assumes the elimination of the unfit, the aged, and all the structurally non-active population) reduce their leisure and rest time to the minimum compatible with survival; their adaptation to variations in the economic apparatus is to be perfect and immediate (which means a perfect aptitude for changing their residence, employment, and qualifications). It is within this perspective that the question of free labour must be considered. There is no necessary or essential link between the capitalist system and free labour. There are historical examples of enterprises based on servile man-power: the silver-mines of Laurium, the great agricultural enterprises of Republican Rome analysed by Cato the elder, the factories within certain concentration camps. It is possible to conceive of an industrial society organized according to these models. However, they would suffer from two major handicaps in terms of efficiency. First of all, the greater the element of constraint in labour and the more this labour is made meaningless for the labourer, the greater the importance of restraints. In other words, the productivity of slaves is too low. In addition, this system can only appear sporadically and temporarily, in periods when the inefficiency of this

factor of production is compensated by its low price, which is to say, by its superabundance (for example, the Roman conquests, the slave-trade, Nazi Europe). As the price of slaves rises, because of their increasing scarcity, the profitability of the enterprise falls, and so economists have been able to show, with a kind of macabre humour, that in the states of the American South it was the slaves who exploited their masters. A second handicap of slavery is found in the excessive rigidity of the labour market. Free labourers, on the other hand, automatically apportion themselves as a function of the needs of the production apparatus (or, in the absence of its needs, they become unemployed). This kind of distribution cannot be achieved with the same measure of efficiency and speed by any planner, even if he has the help of electronic computers. Thus there is no question of denying that freedom of labour plays a role in the industrial system, but one cannot accord it the central role that Marx and, in the end, Weber as well, give to it. In my opinion, freedom of labour is an aspect, but only one among others.

4. That *the absorption of production* by the social organism suffers no impediments, which assumes perfect elasticity of individual and collective demands, with every new discovery creating without delay a corresponding demand. One can conceive of several kinds of societies fulfilling this condition: one curbing individual satisfaction to the maximum for the benefit of collective satisfactions (armaments, monuments, socio-cultural achievements and so on), another making the opposite choice, and a third pursuing both directions at once.

5. That these four conditions are submitted to *no limitation* of any kind: neither *cultural* (habits of consumption can constitute a serious restraint: it is practically impossible to make a population habituated to a diet of bread quickly develop a taste for rice, even though in terms of efficiency it may be necessary at a given moment to devote every effort to rice production), nor *moral* (profit-seeking is an evil, or perhaps leisure is the supreme value), nor *intellectual* (curiosity can lead the mind to concentrate on problems other than those that deal with efficiency). Nor can there be any *political* limitation, for it is necessary that the confrontation of efficiencies be done freely, in a free market. This means that the market must take over the whole world for every limitation is an obstacle to this confrontation and, from this fact, threatens to maintain a lower level of efficiency. The most efficient system thus,

is the one that establishes perfect competition on a world scale. And finally, there can be no *social* obstacle: the search for efficiency will perforce mean momentary suffering. Every measure that is undertaken to limit suffering will, by this fact, limit efficiency as well.

Such a society does not exist and probably never will. I have not claimed to describe an existing society and even less an ideal one, but to establish whatever traits necessarily come to the fore in a society where the search for economic efficiency is pushed to its limit.

All these traits are simply the general conditions for perfect competition such as has been analysed by classical and neo-classical economists. In keeping with my general thesis about human activities, the fact that such a society does not exist means that, up to now, every society has placed obstacles in the way of the pursuit of economic efficiency. This has been done either in a general fashion, by retarding economic activity as much as possible, or only by repressing such and such an aspect of the model (the entrepreneur, technology, labour, inelasticity of demand, limitation of the market, etc.). However, all societies have not established the same obstacles, which gives a precise scale for classifying societies in terms of their economic activities. One society has gone the greatest way in getting rid of all obstacles, western society. Consequently, when all is said and done, the question that I have been pursuing so long about the origins of capitalism must be put in these terms: *Why has western civilization and it alone, removed the obstacles that limit the pursuit of economic efficiency?*

As we see, the great difficulty in social science is to ask the right question: once the question is *constructed* the answer is, in general, easy to obtain. In fact, my work from this point on will be relatively easy. It will be enough to locate the *specific* aspects or facts in Western history which explain that, in the West, each term of the model that I have just set forth has been actually produced in a greater degree than it has in other societies. To show that I am not the victim of an ethnocentric illusion, I will make every effort, in each instance, to determine if other societies have not fulfilled the same conditions with the same consequences. At the end of the analysis it must appear that either the West is the only society to have fulfilled all the conditions demanded by the model, or that one or two conditions (the others having been found to be without decisive consequences) have been determinative.

Part Three
The Genesis of Capitalism

Six: *The Genesis of the Bourgeois*

Henri Pirenne was right to argue that the secret of Western society must be sought in those centuries that made the transition between the ancient world and the Middle Ages. Something extraordinary took place between the fifth and the tenth centuries, a remarkable decline in population, in cultivation of the land, in men's general horizons, and an unbelievable dissolution of political power and of the force of arms. My purpose here is not to explain this decline (which, it must be added, only took place in the Western provinces of the Roman Empire), nor to settle the question of whether blame should be placed on the Barbarian invasions (Piganiol's thesis), on the internal contradictions of the Roman system (Rostovtseff's thesis), or on the Muslim conquest of the Mediterranean basin (Pirenne's thesis). Let us simply consider the economic scene as it appeared in the ninth and tenth centuries, the darkest era of Western history. It is impossible to provide population figures: what is certain is that occupation of the land between the Atlantic and the Elbe and between the North Sea and Sicily was very much reduced. Planted fields must have been seen as clearings in the midst of an immense forest, oases amidst vast empty spaces. Trade was reduced to its most simple expression: the market was confined to the exchange of small surpluses between villages within quite limited areas. Only a few luxury goods (silks, gems, and slaves), which were confined to a few great nobles, were then carried in long-distance trade run by several marginal groups: Easterners, Jews, Cahorsins, Venetians. The cities upon which ancient civilization had been raised were dead or dying. The only ones that managed even to vegetate, and maintained their role as centres of human interaction were essentially episcopal cities. Rome, which, according to Carcopino, had a population of two million during the days of Antonines, by the ninth century could count barely twenty thousand and it was by far the largest city in the West. Herds grazed peacefully amid the grandiose ruins of imperial fora.

The political world provided the same desolate picture. The Carolingian Empire was but a passing realization of a desperate dream of restoring Christianity. A scarcity of material means prevented the constitution of large or permanent armies. The great distances involved made a centralized and effective administration impossible, which is to say, reinforced the autonomy of local courts (the establishment of *missi dominici* was an inevitable and astute, but ineffectual solution). After the brief reprieve during the reign of Louis the Pious, a reprieve resulting entirely from chance (he was the sole heir), the division of the Empire at Verdun between Lothar, Louis the German, and Charles the Bald launched a process that nobody could have checked and that ended with the pulverization of power into a multitude of quasi-sovereign units. The weakenss of political power was revealed in several striking episodes. In 854, in the Loire valley, it was necessary to concentrate the flower of 'French' chivalry under the direction of Robert the Strong in order to defeat a wretched lot of Norse pirates; towards the end of the tenth century, after decades of futile efforts, a quasi-general mobilization was needed to dislodge a handful of Saracens settled in Le Freinet who, from this fortress, had for a century and a half preyed upon Provence and the Rhone valley. It was, in fact, the extraordinary weakness of the arms that opposed them that alone explains the incessant and devastating incursions of Northmen, Saracens and Magyars.

It was possible to fear for a complete and utter disappearance of the West if two institutions had been unable eventually to achieve success. First of all was the Church, the only corporate organization and one which transmitted the idea of the originality of the West as a community with a special destiny. Thanks to the Church a cultural basis was preserved in spite of everything, and, after the storm, it was able to begin reconstruction. And second was feudalism, which, however it may displease Marxists, was not the epiphenomenon of a production system. Feudalism was based on the oath of fidelity that hierarchically bound two men together: the subordinate or vassal, made an oath of allegiance between the hands of his Lord, the most important implication of which was to assure him of the aid of his arms in time of conflict. For his part, the Lord promised aid and assistance to his liege man and, in order to allow him to subsist and maintain a horse and arms, he gave him a fief, which is to say, the revenues of a specific area, which was the only possible source of revenue. It is important to state here that if the feudal tie was hierarchic it nevertheless bound two free men, who were essentially equal and who entered freely into the bond. The meaning of this institution[1] is clear: it was a desperate, but singularly successful solution to the general insecurity that adjusted political power to restricted resources. In fact, such a social organization is conceivable only in the absence of a strong central power able to enforce respect by its administration of the law. At the level of individuals, this was expressed in the law of the jungle and the over-arching need to survive by seeking protection beside a man a little stronger than the others. This is why the beginnings of feudalism always appear when the central power disappears from the midst of an established political unit, as for example in the decline of Egypt, Japan at the end of the Heian era (the end of the eleventh century), or in certain Latin American countries. A desperate need for security was found among the lower echelons of society, within the masses of peasants. Far from being a shameless exploitation of the peasantry, serfdom was a coherent system and appropriate to the circumstances, as it guranteed the masses defence against the incursions of pillaging bands, both barbarian and Christian. As for their being bound to the soil, it is hard to imagine that it was resented an intolerable servitude in a world where changes were practically non-existent and where moving must have appeared to be a terrifying adventure.

The contraction of human interaction, the generalized insecurity and the order that was born from this situation gave rise in this way to a wholly original social organization characterized by three and only three social categories: the clergy, responsible for governing relations with the sacred and the sole bearers of intellectual culture, the nobles, who devoted themselves to political and military activities, and finally the people, who provided for the needs of the whole by their labours in the fields and as artisans. Or rather, the originality does not lie so much in these three categories as in the complete absence of any

---

[1] Or better, of what was much later to become an institution in the hands of jurists who, desiring to aid in the reconstruction of strong and unchallenged monarchies, invented the feudal pyramid where the hierarchy of allegiances culminated in the oath of the great barons in the hands of the king, the suzerain of suzerains, responsible to God alone.

merchants, both in reality and in the conception that society eventually gave itself. Consequently, the first original feature, which appears to me to be crucial for the subsequent evolution of the West, is the constitution of a society conscious of forming one broad unity, Christendom, but which was totally without any social group in charge of trade.

Let us be sure we have grasped the originality of this situation and its unique characteristic. The memory of the Empire and the Church led to a consciousness of being a single unit, at least in principle. Thus the West did not constitute a simple juxtaposition of segments brought together or dispersed according to the fluctuations of politics. These segments represented potential elements of a much broader order whose basis had been defined in terms of cultural and religious considerations. Now, a complex society is held together by more than culture. Political and economic considerations are also important, which is to say, a certain division of labour implying obligations of exchange must also prevail and be enforced. The Roman Empire had represented the most perfect realization of these three exigencies and the European West kept a nostalgia for this unity that guaranteed its greatness.

Such a situation was highly unstable. Whether as a result of a weariness brought on by annual raids or a political awakening (the settlement of the Norsemen under Rollo along the lower Seine by the treaty of Saint-Claire sur-Epte in 911 or the victory of Otto over the Magyars at Lechfeld in 955), there were internal changes about which we know very little, but which were sufficient to alter the general situation. Insecurity diminished, political power was restored at least in the sense of a revival of a central organization, and trade picked up again. Thus is explained the economic 'miracle' of the eleventh century, a crucial turning-point of the West, far more important than that of the seventeenth or even the nineteenth centuries. The accidental depression brought about by the dislocation of the Emipre had been so profound that only two outcomes were possible: disappearance or resurrection.[2] It was probably thanks to the Church that this second outcome resulted. But it did not give rise to a new social order: these

[2] I believe there are situations in the life of societies that are absolutely crucial, beyond which they disappear or find in themselves sufficient reserves of energy to start again in the face of new circumstances. In general these situations are brought on by battles to which a specific date may be affixed. Cheronece and Zama seem to me to be the *termini ad quos*. The originality of the late Middle Age is to have prolonged this decisive period for several centuries. This outcome of events recalls that of Greece from the twelfth to the eighth centuries, after the Dorian invasions.

dark centuries no doubt bequeathed a spiritual order, but also a profound political and economic disorder.

Let us look first at the economic disorder that was to create the bourgeois. The originality of the Western city has been admirably analysed by Max Weber in *Economy and Society*.[3] Let us recall the essential aspects. What distinguished radically the Western city from all others, both in antiquity and in the Middle Ages (and cities are found in all complex societies), is that it constituted a community comprised of free individuals. The fundamental reason for this original feature is the absence of a bureaucratic state power that included the cities and freely quartered its armed forces in them. Max Weber did not give an ultimate explanation for this particularity. For what it is worth, I would advance the following: During the Middle Ages the dislocation of the Roman Empire accounts for it. For ancient Greece it was almost certainly the Dorian invasions that destroyed from top to bottom the Mycenean principalities but without replacing them with a bureaucratic empire. Afterwards followed at least four centuries as dark as those of the Middle Ages with a nostalgia for an original culture here as well, this time expressed in the Homeric poems. Under this hypothesis the Greek city appears as a political form appropriate to the effective dispersal of power coupled with a cultural level that transcended this dispersal. At the same time, such an hypothesis would explain the short life of the cities, soon to be swallowed within an empire. The city that survived into the Macedonian, Hellenistic, and Roman Empires changed its meaning and its purpose by losing the greatest part of its political activity and, more particularly, by losing the right to decide as a sovereign body the questions of peace and war. The decisive fact, therefore, is that from the beginning the Western city appeared able to arm itself. Thus, it was composed of citizen-soldiers who identified with no political body beyond the city. In ancient Greece no political power capable of including all the cities ever existed. The Middle Ages, on the other hand, maintained, at least *in posse*, much broader political units that could be transformed into more or less centralized monarchies. The consequences were of the greatest importance:

Medieval city autonomy rested on different conditions from those of Antiquity. The more typical the ancient city, the more its ruling

[3] II, ix, 8, 2 *et seq.* Published separately as *The City*, tr. and ed. Don Martindale and Gertrud Neuwirth (London: Collier-Macmillan, 1958). References are to this edition.

strata, its capitalists, and even its burghers were politically and militarily oriented (pp. 210–11). . . . To summarise: from the time of the creation of hoplite discipline the ancient polis was a warrior's guild (p. 220).

On the other hand:

Under the domination of the guild the medieval city was pressed in the direction of industry on a rational economic model in a manner alien to the city of Antiquity throughout the period [of] the independent polis. . . . The [urban] citizens had sufficient military strength to sustain the integrity of the inland city, but not to serve as a basis for economic gain. The seat of highest militarism did not lie in the cities, which were in process of developing rational economic means (pp. 223–4).

The essential point, therefore, is the appearance of cities that little by little found themselves dispossessed of every kind of political and military activity, condeming the bourgeois to devote themselves entirely to economic activities. The proof *a contrario* of the decisive importance of this development for the subsequent evolution of cities is provided by the actual history of cities that had the possibility of developing an important political activity. Venice, Genoa, Florence, the Hanseatic cities, all had to wait centuries before being incorporated into the surrounding political units. All these cities, whatever their wealth, whatever the importance of the economic areas they controlled, lacked capitalism and the successive revolutions that the Western economic system experienced. I know the obvious objection: the decline of these cities from the sixteenth century is explained by the discovery of America and the disaplacement of the economic gravity of the West towards the Atlantic. That is, of course, the standard view, and it has the appearance of obviousness: the Atlantic does play an increasing role. But this kind of evidence must be used with caution for the distances involved are relative. It is not at all clear that Genoa is very much closer to America than Seville nor Hamburg than Amsterdam. What is much more significant is that later, the only countries that profited over the long term were countries that had a strong political organization. Above all these were France and England, in contrast with Spain and Portugal, which rapidly were swamped by the enormous increase in the circulation of currency. In other words, it seems to me that historians could revise their ideas about the displacement of economic activities toward North-West Europe. They should relate the discovery of new maritime routes to the appearance of strong centralized States. As I have already had occasion to state, the great rhythms of western economic history, and probably world history, seem to me to have to be related to political phenomena and not the other way around, as is nearly always done. Thus I would maintain the position that the destiny of Venice and Florence, to speak only of them, was, in the modern era, sealed: they declined from the moment they became imperial capitals, at the time when their political activities reached their highest level. Inversely, it is appropriate to note that it was England after the Norman conquest that most fully agreed with this model: royal unification and an end to external danger led to the complete disappearance of the military role of cities.

If cities appeared from the time that society attains a complexity sufficient to demand centres of human interaction (politics, administration, religion, commerce), and if this is true everywhere, the ancient and medieval city is unique. The closest form to the Greek city is the Mesopotamian town. As the Greek, it was the centre of an autonomous politics with, however, two well-known differences. The first is the permanence of the contrast between the urban and rural populations, a contrast punctuated by conflict and the obstinate refusal of country-dwellers to allow themselves to be incorporated into empires. In contrast, the Greek city was simultaneously urban and rural. A second, less decisive difference was the tendency for Mesopotamian cities to be transformed into imperial capitals, with, nevertheless, a remarkable perseverance in defeat. This difference is less important for the Greek cities; Athens, for example, also had imperial ambitions. To exaggerate only slightly, one could say that the Greek city was a complete politico-social organism while the Mesopotamian one was a kind of invading cyst, badly tolerated by the environment.[4]

The Chinese town offers us a radically distinct structure. It constitutes the place where imperial power is exercised by way of mandarin intermediaries and it is entirely without administrative autonomy. In this way it makes a remarkable contrast with the villages that partly escape from imperial power and have their own administration based upon kinship-relations.[5]

[4] A. Leo Oppenheim, *Ancient Mesopotamia: Portrait of a Dead Civilization* (Chicago and London: University of Chicago Press, 1964), pp. 109–42.
[5] Max Weber, *The Religions of China: Confucianism and Taoism*, tr. and ed.

It will be objected, quite rightly, that this is not enough. Every complex society, as I have already shown, has been familiar with a social group entirely devoted to economic activity, or, more precisely, to trading. Thus, it is necessary to introduce an additional original factor of the medieval West. And we have already noted this feature: *the organization of medieval society had not provided for the merchant.* Thus, the merchant provided a double problem: on the one hand, a place in the sun had to be made, and on the other, a principle of identity had to be found. He resolved the first problem by himself, since merchants fulfilled a function of ever-increasing necessity within a society where trade ceaselessly increased. The second problem, on the contrary, took centuries to find its solution. As the supreme values of western society had been noble and ecclesiastical, a man devoted to the accumulation of gain undertook an illegitimate activity. The only way to be recognized by others was, at first, to mimic the higher orders, and later, to join them by being ennobled and acceding to a noble way of life characterized by possession of land and income from rents. As a result, over the centuries the higher levels of the bourgeoisie were constantly being skimmed off in order to pursue non-economic activities. On the other hand, where economic activity was valued for its own sake the bourgeoisie underwent a much more intense development. Thus, in my view, one must reconsider the celebrated relationship that Max Weber established between the Protestant ethic and the spirit of capitalism. The Protestant ethic did not serve so much to confer rationality upon economic activity as to give the bourgeois the feeling that their way of life was legitimate. The instance of the United States is a particularly good example. Their destiny was decided not so much by the Protestant ethic as by the absence of noble and ecclesiastical values. The bourgeois, having no one to imitate, followed his own law. The white slave-owning society of the American South, on the other hand, was impregnated with values of a nobility and lacked an industrial revolution.

It would be false to argue that only Western capitalists desperately sought to escape their condition. This tendency is probably universal. To take but one example, in Japan before the Meiji restoration—and I will have to return to the curious analogies between Japan and the

Hans H. Gerth (Glencoe: The Free Press, 1951), pp. 90-1. The Weberian interpretation is confirmed by Etienne Balazs, *Chinese Civilization and Bureaucracy: Variations on a Theme*, tr. H. M. Wright, ed. Arthur F. Wright (New Haven and London: Yale University Press, 1964), pp. 66–78.

West—capitalist activities were held deeply in contempt and merchants were forbidden to carry swords, to take the names of samurai, or to enter the aristocracy surreptitiously. Of course, they succeeded in avoiding these prohibitions and attained the desired social mobility either by purchasing lands of samurai or daimio who had fallen into poverty or by adopting the sons of nobles in return for large payments. This contrasts with the Western technique, which consisted in marrying a bourgeois daughter to a noble. The universally low esteem accorded to commercial activities was a problem. A simple hypothesis would consist in saying that it followed from the fact that, by nature, the merchant produced nothing and did not contribute to social activities by any tangible way. From one point of view, because he was an intermediary who, until quite recently, satisfied the demands of a tiny elite, he appeared to the common people as a parasite. But, from the point of view of those he served he was a subordinate (but indispensable) factotum. Apart from the unhappy consciousness that this situation instilled in capitalists themselves, it explains a frequently noted characteristic: capitalist activities being reserved for, or cornered by, marginal or pariah groups such as Jews, or the Parsees of Bombay.

To summarize this development, I would say that the genesis of the bourgeois is explained by several original features of Western evolution from the late Middle Ages: (a) an almost complete disappearance of ordered human interaction, (b) the formation of a social system adapted to this situation that did not include the merchant, (c) the re-birth of cities, now stripped of every political and military function and, because of this, forcing their members into economic activities, and (d) the illegitimate nature of these activities forced the bourgeois either to assimilate into legitimate orders or to make his own values triumphant.

Thus did Western society produce this bizarre individual, the bourgeois, devoted exclusively to profit and fundamentally dissatisfied because his way of life was not recognized by society and because it was impossible for him to attain dignity without repudiating himself. He became more and more rich and more and more powerful, but could do nothing with his power.

Now the problem is to know how these men progressively succeeded in increasing their influence to the point of dissolving the old social order. For, one can conceive of a stable society that would confine bourgeois activities within a modest role, sufficient to accomplish the trade that every complex society presupposes, but no more. The

F

problem, therefore, centres upon the multiplication and amplification of these functions, on the constitution of an ever wider market, not only in terms of the area covered but above all in terms of the progressive transformation of use-values into exchange-values.

Seven: *The Genesis of the Market*

At this point one runs the greatest risk of going round in circles, for the extension of the market presupposes the extension of economic activities, and these latter rest upon the former. One may turn these propositions around as one wishes, but so long as one remains within the realm of economics, there is no solution. Thus, one must leave it: let us turn towards politics.

I have said that the Western bourgeois was born from the disorder introduced into feudal society by the resurgence of human interaction beginning the eleventh century. In the same way, I think that the constant expansion of the market, both in extensiveness and in intensity, was the result of an absence of a political order extending over the whole of Western Europe. This situation had decisive consequences for the external as well as the internal economy.

1. *Large-scale international commerce.* It may be agreed that there is no perfectly stable society, that all societies experience change, but also that they do so with widely variable rhythms. The stability, even the relative stability of a social group rests upon the stability of its religious, cultural, political, economic, etc., institutions and upon the order that regulates exchanges (of women, information, goods, commandments, etc.). The greater the regulation of these exchanges the more the rules constitute a coherent system, and the lower the threat to stability. Now, it is reasonable to assume that every social group tends to persevere in its own being. That is to say, it tends to elaborate that system

of rules which guarantees stability and tends, by diverse procedures, to eliminate every disturbing element. If, in consequence, human groups were never in contact with one another, humanity would, no doubt, undergo change, but with infinite slowness. In fact, the only constant and effective possibility for inducing instability is contact: by war, by borrowing, or by trade. These, then, I would say are the international relations that constitute the foundation of the historical evolution of human societies.[6]

Let us return to capitalism. Within a *unified* and stable political whole, the social order has time to establish rules that, in the diverse settings of human activity, guarantee stability.

In the realm of economics, this means that, within any given society, there is a definite conception and a definite organization of labour. The number and quality of manufactured objects are specified and the fraction of production available for trade is very nearly constant. In short, the market is stable. This does not mean that it is forcibly restricted: one may conceive of a stable society where 100 per cent of production would be traded. Now, what is peculiar to the West is that, for more than a thousand years, it has never succeeded in even beginning to construct a political order, first of all European and then, starting in the sixteenth century and reaching a climax in the nineteenth, a world order. This example is nearly unique (I say nearly unique because there is a Japanese parallel to which I will revert in a few pages) in universal history: a society based upon the same moral and material civilization that never ended up in political unity, in short, in an Empire. This phenomenon is peculiar not to the West in general, since there was Alexander and the Romans. It belongs only to the West emerging from feudalism. During the feudal centuries (roughly from the fifth to the tenth centuries), Western men had lived drawn in upon themselves, without significant political ties. When the resurrection of social life burst upon them, particularisms (and especially linguistic ones, as had been clear as early as the acts of the Partition of Verdun in 843) had had enough time to become deeply established, so much so that the resurgence of political power was exploited by narrow, sovereign, and mutually hostile political units.

[6] Need I add that I refuse to fall back upon the procedures of philosophies of totality? No more than did Max Weber claim to replace the economy by religious systems in order to explain, in the final analysis, human societies, do I wish to replace it with external politics. I am simply saying that it would not be without interest to start from this point and see how far it deserves analysis.

Every attempt at establishing a Western political order has been frustrated: the Germanic emperors, the popes, the Hapsburgs, Napoleon, William II, Hitler, and the European Economic Community. According to one's preferences, this persistance in disorder or anarchy will provoke despondency or admiration. There is nothing astonishing about it, and it is easily explained. Every political unit tends simultaneously to preserve its independence and to extend itself externally. When an international system includes numerous political units (what Raymond Aron calls a multipolar and homogeneous system), there is no chance at all for any one of the units to attain sufficient power to create an empire by absorbing the other units. In fact, the relation of forces is such that the coalition of threatened units is always strong enough to beat the ambitious one. Thus, the system tends toward equilibrium as a result of the formation and dissolution of alliances, and this equilibrium means the perpetuation of the division into sovereign units. There is at least one exception which, early on, bothered Clausewitz: Poland, which had entirely disappeared during the eighteenth century. Clausewitz avoided the problem by declaring that the Poles were not Europeans but Tartars who had wandered into the West by mistake. Let us say instead that independence presupposes a minimum of will and the capacity of the elite to overcome its internal difficulties. Such a system will persist so long as the internal struggles that define it do not lead to suicide through the reciprocal exhaustion of all the allies *cum* adversaries thereby leaving it open to a bold Barbarian. The Peloponnesian war opened the way for the Macedonians; the European wars have benefited neither the Mongols, nor the Turks nor, up to now, the Russians.

The consequences of this political situation for the economy are plain, for the absence of political order prevents all economic order. In fact, the international market is necessarily and ruled only by what are eventually purely economic mechanisms (the balance of payments, for example, up to 1914). International trade is ruled by the law of efficacy: the strongest in one given sector prevailing in it over the others (cf. Ricardo's law of comparative advantage).

I have already noted that the peculiarity of economic activities is to be without any internal checks: in international relations there are no checks of any kind. This seems to me to explain the fact that large-scale international commerce, from the eleventh century right up to our own day, has dominated all economic activities and constitutes the main regulator of the great business cycles. The twentieth century is particularly illuminating. Governments responded to the great depression of 1929 by a series of measures that had the consequence of restricting international trade. The result was that the crisis was perpetuated until the war. In 1945, the memory of the depression and Keynes' 'general theory' (which had finally come to the notice of politicians) led governments to intervene in economic life so as to obtain simultaneously full employment and mastery over the business cycle. For a good twenty-five years these objectives have nearly been realized. But, to the surprise of nearly everyone, like a free gift from Adam Smith's 'invisible hand', a rapid increase in national revenue and a massive development of international trade has also been achieved. The surprise and the miracle disappear if, as I believe, the order of the facts involved is reversed and if the success of the western economy from 1945 until the sixties and early seventies is attributed to the extension of international trade. Thanks to the Marshall Plan, the establishment of the Common Market, and the external liberalization of the American market, the political checks of international commerce have been lifted and this has led to a sort of economic explosion whose other aspects are consequences, not causes.

International commerce cannot undergo a continuous development and, at least in tendency, an indefinite one *except where sovereign political units coexist within a culturally homogeneous area.* This last point is of the utmost importance. Trade only attains a decisive importance within a culturally homogeneous area. At the frontiers of these areas, trade can only be concerned with luxury goods (gems, precious cloths, rare animals, ivory, and so forth). This is why these marginal exchanges are always left to marginal groups: Phoenicians, the Egyptian ports of the Red Sea, Palmyra, oases on the silk routes, adventurers (a major factor in all colonization since the sixteenth century), colonial banks and chartered companies. All these phenomena are but buds, outgrowths from an economic system that do not serve as its foundation. This consideration allows us to put colonization in its proper place, which some theoreticians say is the basis of capitalism. The discovery of America and its precious metals no doubt stimulated economic activity. Above all, it utterly ruined Spain. A counter-proof may be drawn from the examples of Greek, Roman, Muslim, Mongol, and Turkish conquests, which liquidated enormous capital hoards, led to important economic activity, occasionally ruined the metropolitan economy, but did not lead to Western capitalism. The decisive role of the several waves of Western colonization for the emergence of Western capitalism is a myth that, in the West, nourishes a guilty conscience, and is tied to the most primitive kind of nostalgia as well as to the emotions of beautiful souls. In other words, it is a handy and reassuring way of foisting one's own insufficiencies upon others.

In the end, all that is plain enough. Just as two men can only exchange their views if they speak the same language, so too can two economic systems communicate only if they are based on the same rules. If not, there is either no trade at all or else the destruction of the weaker by the stronger. In fact, colonization has only been important where it has led to a spatial expansion of the capitalist system: the United States, South Africa, Australia. In short, in all the so-called settlement colonies.

Consequently, the ultimate explanation of the extension of economic activities in the West is the amount of shift between the homogeneity of cultural space and the plurality of political units that are part of it. *The expansion of capitalism owes its origins and its raison d'etre to political* *anarchy.* Besides these consequences for international trade, the repercussions of this situation reach the economy by other ways as well. First of all, the State cannot avoid intervening in economic life in order to promote it. From the beginning, the growth of cities in the early Middle Ages and the increasing influence of the bourgeoisie is explained by the use of this new force by the royal power against the great nobles. Without the possibility of mobilizing large and permanent armies, which is to say, without money, the kings would never have been able to win. Thus, internal anarchy inherited from the feudal order was the motor of capitalist expansion. Likewise, on the international scene, sovereign political units saw and still see their political importance as fluctuating in terms of their economic importance since their political weight in large measure is a function of their economic resources. The inevitable intervention of the State in economic activities has had both fortunate and awkward consequences for the economy. These have varied according to whether the State was content to erect the material foundations of prosperity (roads, ports, bridges, etc.) or the institutional foundations (stable currency, suppression of internal tolls and customs) and not to exhaust the country by excessive impositions nor to substitute itself for the economic agents themselves. Collectivism and State management have only succeeded in school text-books (look, for example, at the constantly favourable judgement they give to Colbertism).

International relations are not conducted solely on the basis of the economic implications of the dialectic of power and defence but also in a much broader and more subtle way, by emulation. The plurality of societies within the same cultural whole means that they survey the same field of possibilities in more or less the same way. The desire to be distinguished and to raise oneself to the level of others ensures that a competitive system is less stable in its choices and more varied in its actualizations. This characteristic is quite striking in Western art, thought, and science—and I shall return to it. It cannot but play a favourable role in the economy: in every age from at least the eleventh century on, a high level of wealth (in Flanders, northern Italy, Holland, France, England) has served as a standard and inspired the less wealthy to raise themselves until they were equal to it.

2. *The Autonomy of the economy.* I am not certain that the opening of foreign markets was sufficient to guarantee the expansion of capitalism. The complementary factor of the limitation of political power within each country was also necessary. The reasons why the West experienced political puralism are complex, and to analyse them in detail would take me beyond my present intentions. I tend to see in this development a kind of historical miracle; that is, an historical event of extreme improbability. What I shall do now is simply suggest the directions in which an explanation must be sought. As I argued above, all power tends toward the absolute. If it is not absolute, this is because some kind of limitations have come into play. In the West we may see several limitations. First there is the Church which, because of its transnational status could not be absorbed by the State (for example, the defeat of the Emperors during the Investiture Conflict). Next, are social elites derived from feudalism and not from service to the State, the growth of cities and the bourgeoisie, whose origins I have already outlined. And finally were village communes that were generally autonomous, if not with respect to the local authorities, at least with respect to the State. It goes without saying that those in positions of power at the centre ceaselessly tried to erode these limitations. They never succeeded, and for a reason that also seems to me to be tied to the international system: a limitation of power to act externally and the constant threat of foreign assault (the two characteristics of a multi-polar system) imply that power is also limited internally and must rely on autonomous centres of decision-making and so may use them only sparingly. To which one may add the role of emulation and the canalization of energies and aspirations towards objectives provided

from without. In this area, from the end of the seventeenth century the role of the English model for the political destinies of the West appears to me as being crucial.

This novel situation had direct repercussions upon economic activity by ensuring that the economy would not be absorbed by the State. Entrepreneurs have benefited from a very great latitude within which they may conduct their affairs and, when circumstances allowed, they have even had the possibility of putting pressure on the State to take measures that were favourable to them. To state my thesis in an extreme form, I would say that political liberties have been based upon the economic prosperity of the West. If one considers this proposition seriously, and if one agrees that contemporary State interventions in economic life have non-economic (but social, political, and ideological) justifications, this poposition ceases to be paradoxical and sounds more like a truism. Economic growth is possible only if all opportunities for profit are seen and exploited, and that is possible only if profit-seeking men are left to busy themselves freely. Now, it is unthinkable that the State, whatever it may be, could bring itself to grant such freedom. Among a host of reasons, two seem to me to be fundamental. The first is that, as I have already mentioned, every political power tends to reduce everything that is external to it, and powerful objective obstacles are needed to prevent it from succeeding. The second is that the free play of economic forces tends to induce deep disturbances in the social fabric. These disturbances cannot help but set off violent reactions on the part of groups whose position and style of life is threatened by them. Capitalism is a catalyst that disturbs the balance. Hence, it is feared by political power, which always seeks to control it. In other words, the degree of freedom accorded by a system to economic activities depends upon the limitation imposed by political power. The less that politics meddles in the economy and the more it tolerates disturbances that follow from economic growth (except for intervening on behalf of entrepreneurs in order to repress any opposition), the more the economy will prosper.

I think that this analysis, in spite of its brevity, allows us to understand why it was in England that the decisive step in the evolution of capitalism was taken. If the general political structure of the West was favourable to economic expansion, it would be the most marked in that country where political power was most limited and tolerated the greatest autonomy of civil society. For reasons that appear to me to owe as much to history as to geography, England found itself in this position. The Norman conquest imposed a political order upon England that was characterized by the existence of a central power limited by the feudal autonomy of the barons. As generally happens when a system is exported, feudalism was achieved there in its purity (the same thing happened in Sicily and Palestine, and for the same reasons). Now, through the centuries until 1688, the central power was always shown to be incapable of breaking the autonomy of the social elites. Thus they were able to flourish with a maximum of liberty but without questioning the existence and the necessity of a central power. That is, liberties were guaranteed without sliding into anarchy, which is probably the best definition of a police state. By guaranteeing the country against any new invasion and by allowing it to be involved in the international game with the least possible expense, England's insularity served it well. Their costs were further diminished by the ability of its ruling elites to put continental rivalries to their own uses through the magisterial principle of the *'justum equilibrium'*. The only exception was the Hundred Years War, which defined precisely a period of economic depression.

The reader risks being baffled by the argument I have just tried to make and, if he is ill-disposed towards it, he may attribute it to interpretive folly. However, comparative history brings grist for my mill and consolidates my position. In order to verify my two statements, that fundamental springs of capitalist expansion are, on the one hand, the coexistence of several political units within the same cultural whole and, on the other, political pluralism which frees the economy, I shall take three examples: Byzantium, Imperial China and pre-Meiji Japan.

3. *Verification.* From the seventh to the end of the eleventh century, *Byzantium*[7] provides a good example of a directed economy. It was entirely under the power of the Eparch or Prefect of Constantinople. He controlled directly, and the following were subjected to his ordinances: production and selling, the exercise of certain financial and judicial professions (bankers, money-changers, notaries and lawyers), workshops, stores and shops, and markets. Artisans and wholesale dealers were grouped into corporations, provided with rules and regulations, directed by a syndic, and were strictly supervised by agents of the Eparch who attended to the rigorous application of rules and had the right to punish offenders. Finally, he saw to the limitation of

[7] For details see *Cambridge Medieval History* (1967), II, ii, ch. 20, esp. pp. 25ff.

commercial and speculative profits and eliminated monopolies and accrued profits.

All this meddlesome regulation was, in principle, valid only for Constantinople. But such was the weight of the city within the Empire that the competence of the Eparch was in practice unlimited. That is not all: the State was not content with supervision and regulation, it actively intervened at all stages of economic movement through its monopolies. Monopolies existed over a great number of essential industries, such as the baking of bread. The State had a monopoly over the purchase of luxury goods (raw silk from China, spices from the Indies, perfumes from Arabia, slaves from the Caucasus), which it exercised as soon as they crossed the frontier; there were even State agents who conducted negotiations for these goods. The great markets of the Empire, Constantinople, Antioch, and, before the Arab conquest, Alexandria, were run by the State. And finally, the State itself was a producer, for example of silk goods in the Gynaeceum of the Great Palace. In short, the State dominated the whole of economic life: it regulated, fabricated, bought, sold, kept monopolies to itself, and supervised private enterprises by fixing quality, quantity, price, and wages.

Why this attitude of encroaching? To speak of the traditions of the Lower Empire is not enough, for it would be necessary to explain why the tradition was accepted. The first reason is very simply the existence of a strong and centralized State that tended to absorb all social activities. Here this tendency was reinforced by the necessity to provision the city of Constantinople and to guarantee a minimal activity so that the populous would remain peaceful. It was also reinforced by the needs of the State coffers. To all this must be added an ethical element as well: the desire to *curb the duplicity of merchants*. An anecdote well illustrates the mistrust in which the activities of merchants were held. The Empress Theodora had allowed herself to finance a ship; the Emperor Theophilus (829–42) made her burn it along with its cargo as such activity was beneath the dignity of an Empress.

An organization of this kind was based on a strong central power. From the time of Comnenus at the end of the eleventh century this power began to crumble: at the same time as the monopolies disappeared a free market was formed. *But* this liberation did not benefit Byzantine entrepreneurs. It went instead to the more dynamic foreigners from the Italian merchant republics, who obtained permanent concessions and commercial privileges in Constantinople. This evolution is interesting for it reveals that it is not necessary for a power to be weak in order to free economic activity, but liberal. Political move-ment had brought monopolist Byzantium to decadence and not to pluralism.

The economic history of *imperial China* confirms my hypotheses in a most remarkable way.[8] The Chinese system was characterized by the hold that the State, through the mediation of a class of scholar-bureau-crats, maintained over social life. The most distinctive aspect, as has already been suggested, was the absence of any autonomy in the cities, which were centres of administration. The free play of commercial activity was prohibited by the constant threat of exactions by the bureaucrats and arbitrary intervention by the State. Individuals pre-disposed to, and capable of engaging in, business did exist in China. Likewise, there existed a technical and scientific curiosity sufficient to end up eventually in fundamental industrial change. And finally, there was a substantial accumulation of capital. The hypothesis suggests that as soon as there is any weakening of the central bureaucratic power, that is, as soon as the organization that defined the structure of the whole of Chinese society was removed, a victory of provincial particularism would enable economic activities to spring to life. Economic history entirely confirms this hypothesis. Each time China was politically divided, capitalism flourished. The fact is very clear for the period studies by Balazs, the end of the T'ang and especially during the Song period, the second half of the eighth century to the thirteenth century. The same evolution may be found in the more distant past: the so-called period of Warring Kingdoms (453–221 B.C.), probably the richest and most brilliant of all Chinese history, the period of the Three Kingdoms (A.D. 220–280), and finally the period of the Six Dynasties (A.D. 316–580) when China was divided between the Northern bar-barian kingdoms and the national dynasties of the South. However, even during these favourable periods commercial activities were to be restricted to a certain level by the bureaucratic control maintained in each principality. Consequently both my hypotheses seem to be entirely verified: in order to be born and then to develop, capitalism presupposes the division of a single cultural area into several political units, and, in order to flourish, it presupposes a limited political power within each unit.

The Japanese example furnishes a supplementary and signal proof. *Japan* entered history during the sixth century A.D. with the political

[8] I have relied here on the excellent book of Etienne Balazs, *Chinese Civilizati on and Bureaucracy, op. cit.*

crisis initiated by contact with China.[9] In order to maintain their independence, Japanese elites responded by the formation of a very peculiar kind of central power. The State was to be in the hands of a minority who combined personal rule in the provinces and unification at the Court. This led to an original mixture of centripital and centrifugal forces; in effect, there were two political systems, the one provincial the other central. As for the keystone of the system, the emperor or Tenno, he had no power at all but simply represented the symbol of cultural unity.

This unique organization was maintained in spite of numerous changes over the centuries: there remained permanently a powerless symbol of unity, increasing cultural unification (first in the face of Chinese opposition and then, from the nineteenth century, the West), and a dispersal of power among rival principalities. This situation recalls in a most striking way the western international system. Michel Vié put it very well: 'Japan, with its juxtaposition of autonomous principalities, formed an international society whereby a victorious coalition maintained a *status quo* favourable to itself. The State remained far from being united.' 'Tokugawa Japan never ceased to be internally an international social order.'[10] The Meiji Restoration failed to introduce any substantial modifications into this framework: the emperor stayed powerless; power was exercised by an elite that had a relatively pluralist social background, and was fractured by numerous conflicts; cultural unity was preserved, as was a fierce national independence. In short, there existed a weak state but one sufficiently well defined to respond effectively to foreign challenges.

From the beginning, this political structure led to a flourishing market-economy. Let us recall the principal stages. From the eighth century the Court was the driving force of the market through the expenditure of the surplus on the construction of capitals and the maintenance of the aristocracy. During the eleventh and twelfth centuries, local markets multiplied and commerce among different regions appeared. Guilds of merchant-artisans were formed at Kyoto, Nara, Hakata, and Naniwa (in these last two towns, because Chinese merchants had arrived there). The Middle Age (which refers to the period from the twelfth to the sixteenth centuries) was characterized by an increase in provincial armed forces, which is to say, decentralization

[9] I have used Michel Vié's book, *Histoire du Japon* (Paris: P.U.F., 1969), a remarkable work of precision, intelligence and conciseness.

[10] Vié, *Histoire du Japon*, pp. 96–7, 109.

was accentuated and the aristocracy was enlarged. The economic consequences were obvious. One may note a commercial expansion towards China and the birth of the great autonomous ports: Hakata, Hyogo and above all, Sakai. The market economy extended its influence. It was stimulated by fiscal transfers from the provinces toward the Court and by the growth of centres of taxation and consumption, which was the economic role played by monasteries and *shoen*, or aristocratic estates. Trade re-oriented towns toward the countryside: especially after 1300 the village economy opened up and peasants became committed to the market. As a result of this movement, an increasingly specialized population of merchants and artisans formed the nucleus of the towns and set up their own specific institutions (the *toya* and the *Za*). Only the town of Sakai, however, attained complete autonomy. In the others, at Kyoto, Nara, Hakata and Hyogo, the merchants were able to exercise police functions only within the limits of a single quarter of the towns. From the second half of the fifteenth century on, a network of towns and connecting roads, particularly dense in central Japan, Kansai, was built. Economic expansion was helped by the wars among the principalities for they eliminated the old elites, aided social mobility, and limited fiscal levies.

Between 1560 and 1915, a political reversal re-established a central power without eliminating the traditional pluralism of the elite. Several strong personalities, Oda Nobunaga (1534–82), Toyotomi Hideyoshi (1536–98), and Tokugawa Jeyasu (1542–1636), installed by war the Shogunate regime and inaugurated the Edo era, which lasted until 1871. In order to finance their military exploits these men were in need of a flourishing economic activity. It is remarkable that they were sufficiently aware of the laws of economics to succeed not in absorbing the economy but in freeing it. They encouraged large-scale commerce, freed markets, suppressed tolls, repaired roads and reformed the currency. The results were convincing. International trade was intensified and the market-economy was expanded. To take but one example, at the end of this period, two-thirds of all agricultural production and 30 to 40 per cent of rice production had been commercialized. New categories of capitalists appeared. Big munition makers grew and benefited from wars at the beginning of the period. In the seventeenth century, merchant-bankers were firmly installed in Osaka, armament and wholesale commercial enterprises multiplied, and by 1680 the Mitsui and Sumitomo were securely established. Numerous monopolies were born in the eighteenth century and finally, after 1800, merchants and merchant-entrepreneurs proliferated around the great cities and out into the countryside. From the end of the seventeenth century this economic explosion was enhanced by a demographic explosion tied to the end of the wars and accompanied by a massive agricultural change (thanks to dykes, canals and drainage projects, the amount of land under cultivation was doubled; capital equipment and manure were more widely employed; improved techniques for harvesting rice were introduced and there was a general increase in industrial agriculture, which led to profits and cash payments—all these improvements except for the earliest ones, which were undertaken by the State, were the work of private initiative and individual investments). Population probably trebled. By the eighteenth century, an upper limit was reached: food shortages and famines forced the population to limit its fecundity, by infanticide.[11]

There were two limits to this economic expansion: the custom of working in the shelter of public privileges, and the inaccessibility of public office, which was monopolized by a military elite (from whom came a permanent threat of confiscating the merchants' goods). The question is: was Japan on the way to undertaking a great industrial transformation before having to undergo the opening to the West? It is certain that the Meiji period was not a miracle but a crowning event. A developed agriculture, a market-economy, private capital, a class of active and competent entrepreneurs, a high level of instruction, an open and dynamic elite—all this contributed to making the passage to the industrial age almost natural. Two points, however, incline me to doubt whether contact with the West was useless, or in any case, was unnecessary. First, one must recall the narrowness of the material bases of the Japanese economy. In the absence of a military expansion overseas (which, strictly speaking, must not be excluded) Japan lacked the natural resources in raw materials and sources of energy upon which a native industry could be built. Access to world markets and thus contact with the West appears to have constituted an indispensable condition. A second Japanese characteristic appears to me to have been even more important: economic activity developed within the interstices of a social system that provided only weak checks to it, but *at no time does one notice a fixation with economic matters*, such as took place in the West. The social mobility determined by the economic expansion of the Middle Age did not bring a capitalist bourgeoisie to the social

[11] Akira Hayani, 'Aspects démographiques d'un village japonais 1671–1871' *Annales E.S.C.*, 24 (1969), pp. 617–39.

summit, but the *bushi*, the warrior. The warrior represented the social ideal, the model whom the ambitious strove to copy. Within the Japanese value-system, military and aristocratic values far outstripped economic ones. During the Edo period, the *bushi* were intensely interested in all the new techniques that filtered in from the West. But this curiosity was put to the service of a national pride that can, at this early date, rightly be called nationalism.

Consequently, in my search for peculiarly Western factors, I must consider the extent to which the Western value-system worked to the advantage of economic values and why a kind of gigantic collective transfer was effected upon them.

Eight: *The Genesis of the Entrepreneur and the Technologist*

The eleventh-century bourgeois was not yet an entrepreneur. He was content to organize and multiply exchanges, his profit consisting in the fee he was paid for this service. The moment he took part in the pro- duction of goods available for trade he became an entrepreneur. Thus, the first figure of modern capitalism was the merchant-entrepreneur (who first appeared in the twelfth and thirteenth centuries), who obtained his own raw materials (especially textiles, that is, wool, linen, and a little cotton produced in the eastern Mediterranean basin), had it worked on by artisans (practically always these were peasants, an impediment only in the imagination of theoreticians, since their use avoided the corporations), and then began the process of commercialization. The third stage of the rationalization of the economy began in the eighteenth century, when it was applied to the organization of labour (first in manufacture and then in large mills and factories) and to technological research. Neither the organization of rural artisans in cottage industry, nor manufacture, nor technical progress, were first-order phenomena. They were forms of economic activity that necessarily followed from the industrial spirit, which, in its most general sense, could be defined as the application of rational thought to the economic realm. It follows that all rational thought or activity could contribute to the emergence of the industrial system as soon as it was applied to the economic realm, even when the economy was not envisaged as an end in itself.

Following Max Weber, one may call attention to the role of monks, not only in the West but also in Tibet, Japan, China, and everywhere that strongly structured communities had to manage a capital foundation or, very simply, to ensure their own subsistence. Here is a characteristic passage:

> In that epoch the monk is the first human being who lives rationally, who works methodically by rational means toward a goal, namely the future life. . . . The economic life of the monastic communities was also rational.[12]

The celebrated analyses of the *Protestant Ethic* were in the same vein. We must recall once again that, in this book, Weber related two phenomena in order to show how a religious ethic can act upon certain aspects of one particular brand of capitalism: the spirit, though not the letter of the text, allows the establishment of a relation of cause and effect. Later on in other texts[13] he was much less prudent. There he affirmed with no ambiguity that the Reformation constitutes a turning point of economic history, for it secularized ascesis and transferred it to daily life here below. Pushed to these extremes the theory is at best false, and at worst absurd.

One may multiply examples and show the economic consequences of the successive rationalizations of armies throughout all history. Or again, one may show the economic decline that accompanies various contemporary forms of nationalism. Or finally, there is the economic by-product of the Marxist–Leninist ideology in the Soviet Union. Everywhere there is a striving towards a goal and the rational use of means, the economic apparatus will benefit from it. But capitalism is something quite different. It is not just the rationalization of economic activities, which is found everywhere; above all, it is a unique propensity to apply rational thought to economic activities. And that is what gives us the problem.

I recognize that I am treading upon thin ice, but one must take risks. I pose as a working hypothesis that, while it is not impossible for a man to aspire to Nirvana nor to be nostalgic for his mother's breast, such an inclination may well be hidden beneath a contrary appearance, restlessness. Pascal held that it was in the nature of man to be unable to remain alone in a room, doing nothing, for twenty-four hours.

[12] *General Economic History*, tr. F. H. Knight (London: George Allen & Unwin, 1927), p. 365.

[13] In particular in the *General Economic History*, pp. 365–8.

Although there are innumerable ways of acting or of being active, if an activity is to have consequences for the collectivity, there must be numerous practitioners of it—or at least some who pursue the activity systematically. But such socially effective activities are numerically limited. I can conceive of only four: religion, war, politics, and economics. And so my second hypothesis is as follows: if it is agreed that in every complex society there is a more or less equal distribution of personalities particularly gifted for each of these activities, we may reasonably expect that for whatever reason, the emphasis placed upon one activity among others will, through socialization and selection mechanisms, bring about a relatively greater concentration of gifted individuals in this particular sector. If, inversely, a society tends to devalue one, two, or three activities, it is probable that individuals will be inclined to specialize and perfect themselves within the activities that remain socially attractive. It follows that similar kinds of variations depend strictly upon the kinds of socially attractive activities, and not upon the necessities of survival. The constraints of labour mean that most men may not choose what they wish to do with their life. The choice of an activity is a privilege reserved for elites. It is a small minority who define a civilization, which is the original organization that a society actually brings into existence from a range of possible activities. A small minority make history, for only they have the time to do so. Consequently, I propose to examine to what extent the West has had a tendency to close entry into religious, military and political activities and to direct elites toward economic ones.

1. *The Devaluation of Religious Activities.* We are dealing here with an immense question, one that I can only briefly touch upon here. Had I time enough I would orient my argument along these three directions:

(a) *The separation of Church and State.* This was part of Christianity from the beginning: *Reddite quae sunt Caesaris Caesari, et Dei Deo.* No doubt the progressive Christianization of Roman society ended up with a State religion under Theodeosius, but never did it appear anything like a theocracy (apart from the short-lived attempt of Pope Innocent III). The political power always claimed to dominate and succeeded in dominating the religious power, and used it to its own ends. The significant consequence of this state of affairs was that Western society has always had the possibility of establishing borders between secular and religious activities, which meant the *possibility* existed of confining religion within private life without drawing the whole social order into question. It also meant the *possibility* of tolerating the death of God without the whole civilization falling apart (in contrast with Islamic and Hindu societies, which would be shattered by the disappearance of the religious principle). In other words, the peculiar feature of the West, owing to the original separation of Church and State, was to have included religious unbelief among its possibilities of evolution, but in such a way that its own foundations were not endangered by it.

(b) *Theological thought.* It was unfortunate for Christianity to have appeared in a society where intellectual speculation was fairly widespread and had attained a high degree of refinement. Whether it was in order to defend Christianity against attack or because clerics had themselves been brought up on this thought, almost immediately Christianity was oriented towards the rationalization of the divine message. The consequences of this orientation were serious. Theological thought was able to define itself as a rigorously logical and coherent system based upon one or several revealed postulates (which might be called dogmas). Now, Christianity contained at least two structurally insurmountable ambiguities: the ontological status of Christ and the problem of salvation. The first inflamed passions and led to the improbable conflicts of the fourth century at the time of the Arian controversy. The second tore apart the West during the sixteenth and seventeenth centuries. Let us consider only the first point. That Christ was the son of God raised insurmountable logical problems. In fact, either there is no difference between the two hypostases and Christ is simply God, whence one falls back into Jewish monotheism and so the specific feature of Christianity is destroyed (the Sabellian heresy, taken up later by various forms of monarchianism). Or, Christ was only a man and one falls into other difficulties (the Arian heresy, the anomoeans, and the monophysites). The only way to maintain the originality of Christianity was to propose a solution in between these two extremes. Such solutions were multiple. Between 341 and 351 as many as seven formulae were considered and positions eventally stabilized around the three well-known groups, the *homoousians, homoiousians* and *homoeans*.

 Should a specialist chance to read these lines I hope he will excuse this rather cavalier treatment. I simply wish to suggest that the rational treatment of the data of faith necessarily involves ambiguities and inevitably leads to successive heresies (orthodoxy may be defined as the provisionally dominant heresy). This passion for theological disputation burst forth with renewed force from the eleventh century on, carrying in it the seeds of its own destruction. The constant retraction of its own fundamental postulates or dogmas by theology must one day have led from the Augustinian formulation (*credo ut intelligam*) to the Anselmian (*intelligo ut credam*), before ending up with the sarcasms of unbelief.

(c) *Science.* In a marvellous book, Lucien Febvre has shown that in order for unbelief to have triumphed, it was necessary beforehand to have discovered a new basis for the order of the world. The concept of nature, gradually endowed by science with greater precision, scope, and depth, took the place of faith. Thus, it is only from the seventeenth, and above all, from the eighteenth century that unbelief was able to triumph. It is unnecessary to insist upon this point which is known and acknowledged by everyone. The result of this vast movement, which Max Weber has called the 'disenchantment of the world', was not the disappearance of the religious factor[14] but its confinement within a small part of daily life or within socially marginal groups. The fact is that, since the eighteenth century, the West has never been able to mobilize the populace by an appeal to religious values.

2. *Specialization of the Art of War.* It would be paradoxical to hold that war and military values have disappeared from the West. However, in this realm as well the Western evolution has been unique. The constitution of centralized monarchies resulted in a transference of the use of force to public authority. Internally the consequence has tended to be the elimination of violence (baronial and family feuds, banditry, etc.). Externally, the task of conducting war has been confined to professionals, the cannon-fodder being recruited from the dregs of the European population.

Once again one has an intuition, undemonstrable in itself, that economic activities have become much more intense than the ever-diminishing passion for war. This intuition may be verified by several facts. I have already noted the example of England. Its island position and the subtle balancing game it played on the continent allowed it to reduce its force requirements to the simplest terms: defence was based upon the ultimate rampart, the battle fleet. One of the most

[14] Religion seems to me to constitute a necessary dimension of the human condition, born from consciousness of the horror of death. Whenever a society refuses to grant religion a special sphere within which it may develop, the spiritually inspired turn themselves to other activities: politics, economics, aesthetics, etc.

this is wrong!

important results of this development was the part taken by the nobility in business. In England one does not notice—and this from the time of the consolidation of the Norman conquests—a transformation of the landed nobility into rentiers. Rather, they become entrepreneurs. It is difficult to avoid thinking that the only explanation for this is that it had nothing else to do: the outlet of war was closed to it, the fixed limits to royal power had prevented it being transformed into a parasitical court.

Another significant example, the United States. Apart from the War between the States, the whole of American history to 1914 was characterized by the insignificance of foreign policy and the weakness of the army. Again, one may cite the conspicuous examples of Germany and Japan since 1945, whose astonishing economic expansion in the wake of a crushing military defeat can only be explained by the impossibility, or the refusal, of an active foreign policy. Let us end this review of facts with the most striking example. The decisive phase of Western industrialization is situated between 1815 and 1914, in other words, during a century marked by a stable European equilibrium and by the scarcity or brevity of conflicts, especially between 1871 and 1914.[15]

Western originality in comparison to other civilizations is variable. Sometimes bellicose activities are limited within a society and sometimes they are limited towards the outside. But it is rare indeed that they would be limited in both directions at the same time. For example, owing to its insular position and its will to maintain its independence, Japanese society experienced scarcely any foreign wars until the end of the nineteenth century (one can hardly count the attempted incursion of Korea in the seventh century and the two unsuccessful attempts at invasion by the Mongols in 1274 and 1281 under Kubilai). On the other hand, internal conflicts were almost constant. They were especially ferocious and took the form of wars because of the international structure of the social system. In the opposite direction, the Incas seem to have eliminated all internal conflict but undertook a very active foreign policy. The Chinese empire experienced a more complex

[15] So as to avoid all ambiguity, I should make it clear that the celebrated theses of Saint-Simon, Comte, Schumpeter, and Veblen, which hold that industrial society will eliminate war, are the inverse of mine. In my view, it is in light of the degree to which military values are eliminated or limited, for reasons that have nothing to do with the economy, that industrial society may develop. Peace based upon economic values is only an enticement.

situation. The absence of any threatening neighbours (outside the Barbarians who were every ready to exploit any weakness in imperial power) did as much to keep it from an aggressive politics as did the necessities of defence. The stability of the Chinese world compared to the outside was symbolized by the Great Wall, clearly built as a result of defensive thinking. Hence the almost complete absence from the gallery of Chinese heroes of any military leader and the deep contempt in which the soldier as a social type was held. But then within China conflicts were never lacking: there were wars among principalities during periods of division, peasant wars, bands of brigands and outlaw warlords.

All these observations upon massive civilizational facts are subject to qualification and discussion. However, the originality of the West seems to me to be well established. Especially after the eighteenth century, it succeeded in constructing simultaneously an international order based upon the equilibrium of powers and an internal order that tended to eliminate both public and private violence. The important thing is that this evolution had repercussions in the scale of values, namely a relative devaluation of the military career which turned the most gifted members of society away from it.

3. *The Limitation of Political Activities and the State Apparatus.* I have already shown how this aspect of Western societies contributed in a decisive way to the birth of capitalism. It probably worked in an indirect way as well, by influencing the human resources. Compared to the societies of Greece and Rome, the political organization that emerged from feudalism was characterized by a State apparatus having control over vast areas, whereas in antiquity and even under the Roman Empire, innumerable cities had administered themselves. I would argue that in all likelihood and in spite of an absence of figures, it is probable that the proportion of men who were involved in public affairs was less in the West. If one turns towards monopolistic political systems for comparison, far from being topheavy, the West has the advantage of being rather streamlined. In fact political monopolies have had to develop bureaucracies in order to establish themselves and then to continue to exist. Now it is well-known that a bureaucracy tends to proliferate by itself like a cancer. Since in other places bureaucrats were part of the State apparatus and were in possession of part of its power, they benefited from a prestige that induced the ambitions of new generations to seek satisfaction within the bureaucracy. The Chinese example is the

most obvious: for two thousand years the bureaucratic class continued to drain off the most capable and ambitious young men. Thus it would seem to me to be reasonable, if not established, that the human resources taken up by political and administrative offices has been less in the West than in other societies. But even in the West there are significant differences in the economic system according to the greater or lesser importance of political activities. In places such as the United States, Sweden, Switzerland, or England, where historically the State apparatus has been reduced to its simplest expression and the passion to administer has been limited, economic activity has been more intense than, for example, in France, endowed from the days of the *Ancien Regime* with a proliferating bureaucracy, and, after 1871, with a super-abundance of political personnel. Germany and Italy stagnated for centuries during which time the multiplicity of political centres kept a large fraction of the elite occupied. Economic growth helped forge the bonds of unity whence came a relative reduction in the number of political personnel. I would certainly grant that other factors have played a part in explaining these divergences and that, by and large, the economic results have been comparable in different countries. However, I tend to believe that the roles that society attributes to men, peculiar creatures that they are, are not independent of the social consequences that result.

These few remarks have the aim simply to suggest that the great originality of the West since the eleventh century is little by little to have devalued religious, military, and political and bureaucratic values. So that I shall not be thought so naïve as to claim that this devaluation has been completely achieved, I would once more recall that, in my view, the dimensions of the human condition are multiple, but the relative importance that every civilization attributed to any one of them is variable. Consequently, every civilization *tends* to make certain values privileged and, because of this, canalise energies towards them.

Thus, the original evolution of the West *has tended* to push into the shadows, among all possible social types, the priest, the politician *cum* bureaucrat, and the soldier, in order to endow two types with privileges. These two were decisive factors in industrialization, one devoted to searching exclusively for profit and the other to scientific and technical progress. I would call them the entrepreneur and the technologist. These two categories are connected neither historically nor conceptually. The entrepreneur is a transformation of the bourgeois who we have seen appear as early as the eleventh century. The technologist is the modern reincarnation of the intellectual rationalization that first appeared in Ionia in the sixth century B.C. And these two activities are not necessarily joined together. But, in an economically competitive regime, the use of technical progress is a source of enormous profits. Just as competition always ends by equalizing chances, whether by all the competitors adopting the technical advance involved or by the elimination of those who do not, it also engenders, in turn, a further search for technical progress. This point is too clear to have to insist upon it. Whether scientific and technical research ends up influencing the economy is less clear. We may grasp the problem first at its most general level. Here we would argue that the scientific attitude, like the religious, owes its origins to the vast gap that man witnesses between the frailty of his own being and the terrifying power of his environment. One of the constant directions of human activity has been to bridge this gap either by intellectual constructions destined to give him a conceptual mastery of his milieu,[16] or by technical improvements capable of mastering it materially.

In other words, conceptual and Promethean attitudes (including magic ones) are equally part of the human condition and are joined by unbreakable bonds. The result is that in every society technical equipment and conceptual frameworks are adapted to each other. The weaker the technology the more that magical behaviour will be accentuated. And inversely, the more that thought is committed to the road of scientific efficiency the more will technology also be efficient.

Here again history provides us with facts to confirm this hypothesis. Ever since antiquity intellectual speculation has been accompanied by technical research, and often these have been carried on by the same man, as is symbolized in the person of Archimedes.[17] The entire

[16] Claude Lévi-Strauss seems to me to have touched upon an essential idea in his preface to Marcel Mauss' *Anthropolgie et sociologie*. He suggests that since language was given to man, he has the whole of the realm of possible expression before him. From the beginning, the task of humanity has been to make this available expression coincide with the realm of the expressed, which constitutes the world. The excess of expression that is provisionally not influenced by the specific thing expressed he calls *mana*. Thus there is no gap, at this level, between magic or savage thought and scientific thought.

[17] On the other hand, apart from military applications, his technical curiosity did not result in any notable economic transformation but remained purely speculative. The explanation, it seems to me, need not be sought, as is usually done, in slavery but in the scarcity of entrepreneurs and in the absorption of the Hellenistic Kingdoms into the Roman Empire, which is to say, in the closing of the market.

Renaissance was characterized by an intense curiosity in science and machines, and here the symbolic man would be Leonardo da Vinci. Now, the disenchantment of the western world has been accompanied by an extensive promotion of intellectual speculation, which has found expression (without, however, there being any cause-and-effect relation, for what is involved is an identical orientation) in a feverish interest in technical progress. One may consider, for example, the remarkable academies of the French provinces during the eighteenth century, where may be found men passionately involved in the problems of agronomy, beetroot, sainfoin and alfalfa. There can be no doubt that, in the beginning, this passion was purely disinterested. Japan again may serve to verify my assertion. Starting in the Edo period (the beginning of the seventeenth century), a secularization of thought may be detected. In the Edo academy and in the provincial schools created by the *daimyo* for the use of the *bushi* warriors, a laicised version of Confucianism was taught. It was derived from the commentary of Tchou Hi, a Chinese philosopher of the twelfth century, and emphasized problems of order and social harmony and the identity between nature and society. From social order one may easily pass to natural order, from which derives the great receptivity of the Japanese elite to Western science and technology.

The economic consequences of the disinterested passion for science and technology are inevitable. Let us consider a typical example, agricultural research in Holland, England, and France during the seventeenth and eighteenth centuries. The improvement of methods of cultivation and the development of agricultural techniques capable of removing the old limitations imposed by the necessity of fallow land allowed for an unheard-of increase in production. This tended to mean an increase in the quantity that each labourer produced and thus (apart from demographic and social consequences to which I shall return) the transformation of an increasing proportion of production into exchange value. It follows that from the end of the eighteenth century the ties between technology and the entrepreneurial spirit grew more intimate and ended finally with the veritable fusion of the two that may be observed over the last twenty years.

The collective shift of economic activities may be verified at another level as well. Civilization is a luxury, and presupposes the ability of men to produce more than is indispensable to their survival. This may be stated more exactly by saying that civilization is born from savings men impose upon themselves or that are imposed upon them, since producers need not consume everything they produce. A fraction is saved and freed for any number of uses. A civilization is best defined by the use it makes of this fraction. Ancient Egypt devoted it in part to the foundation of priestly orders whose task was to honour the dead and in part to the construction of temples, tombs, pyramids, and statues intended to make fast a religious and intellectual system in stone and metal. The ultimate goal of the whole social system (and not just for the elite, so far as the texts allow us to estimate popular sentiments) was metaphysical.[18] The Greco-Roman civilization invested its surpluses mainly in the construction and beautification of cities. The Hellenistic and Roman elites practised evergetism, that is, competition among the wealthy in expenditure designed to improve the looks of the city and amuse the people.[19] The medieval and modern West has built villages, towns, monasteries, churches, cathedrals, castles. Since the end of the eighteenth century, and above all during the nineteenth, it was the first society to have systematically diverted the surplus towards productive investments. The tendency of the system has been to increase efficiency so as to enlarge the surplus and the fraction reinvested: the original contribution of the contemporary West to the human adventure is the factory. Factories benefit from a relative priority over all other achievements: monumental constructions, popular amusements, or the maintenance of an idle elite devoted to prayer, war, intellectual speculation, aesthetic emotions, or sensual pleasure. Whatever may be the sentiment upon which this basic change rests, it is undeniable and manifests in a shocking way a most profound and unexpected alteration in the scale of values.

[18] The expression is of François Daumas, *La Civilisation de l'Égypte pharaonique* (Paris: Arthaud, 1967), pp. 244–6.

[19] Cf. the excellent article of Paul Veyne, '*Panem et circenses:* L'évergetisme devant les sciences humaines', *Annales E.S.C.*, 24 (1969), pp. 785–825.

Nine: *The Genesis of the Labourer and the Consumer*

The model of a society perfectly efficient within the economic realm, such as I have constructed in section Five, is slowly being put into place. I have shown how the West has produced the bourgeois, the expanding market, the liberation of the economy from politics, the entrepreneur, and the technologist. All that is left before the picture is completed is to bring to light the genesis of the labourer and the consumer. These two elements raise hardly any problems.

We recall the two principal characteristics of an ideal labourer: a life devoted entirely to labour and a perfect adaptability to variations in the machinery of production. It is also necessary that there be a sufficient number of labourers. The only point that really is a problem, as Marx rightly saw, is to know where the first entrepreneurs found their manpower. Marx got himself entangled in inextricable difficulties, whereas the solution is really very simple. It is enough to recall that the agricultural labourer, for quite natural reasons, is bound to a very specific rhythm. Except for highly specialized and localized produce, such as the vine, agricultural labour is concentrated in specific limited periods during the year: sowing, mowing, and harvesting. These tasks require a set amount of time and arms. But between these busy periods the demand for labour falls off. The result, on the average, is a considerable surplus of available labour-time in agricultural areas compared to the amount of time actually required for agricultural labours properly speaking; in certain agrarian systems this gap can be enormous. For example, growing rice in paddies requires, on average, about 140 days a year. But during peak periods, the quantity of manpower needed to accomplish the required tasks represents a population density of from 500 to 1,000 a square kilometre. Thus one gets an idea of the considerable quantities of labour-time available in the countryside for other tasks.

In every agrarian society, this non-peak labour-time is devoted to several different jobs that, for simplicity, we will call artisan work (often, as in China or the Indies, may be found a genuine specialization of villages in one kind of production or another, which amounts to commercialization). One may see that the system of the merchant-entrepreneur had no trouble entering the village-based 'labour-market' and diverting part of this available time to its own profit. In so doing it had no need to destroy serfdom, first of all because serfdom never involved the whole population (there always existed freeholders, even if the historian is unable to calculate the proportion of the population involved), but above all, because the landlord saw a role for himself in the exploitation of the serf by the entrepreneur, through the mediating factor of his rents. Thus, all rigid and juridical conceptions of social systems must be abandoned, for societies are always much more flexible than they appear in textbooks.

The extension and expansion of capitalism depended upon the integration of the increasingly strong masses of labourers into the new system. In this way the reserve of labour, which had served from the eleventh to the eighteenth century, was shown to be insufficient. It is at this point that basic changes in agriculture took place, the primary condition for industrial transformation. The increase in agricultural productivity freed masses of labourers who had neither capital nor land and who, for decades, had haunted the countryside (as for example in the Great Fear of 1789) before being gradually absorbed into industry. The West, above all, experienced a unique demographic evolution. From the eleventh century it experienced three fundamental shifts. After the depopulation of the late Middle Ages, a veritable population explosion may be observed from the eleventh to the thirteenth centuries at the end of which, France, for example, had brought more land under cultivation than it has ever done since. Then, for the next two centuries, catastrophies succeeded one another (plague, war, famine), followed by two centuries of unstable equilibrium (especially during the seventh century, which, demographically speaking, was very dark indeed). And then, from the eighteenth to the beginning of the twentieth century, population growth was extraordinary. Historical demography is still in its infancy so that any explanation of these cycles can only be hypothetical. Nevertheless, it seems highly probable that western behaviour in the field of procreation need scarcely have varied until the nineteenth century, which is to say that the natality rate has hardly changed at all. Thus mortality rates must explain the cycles. This poses hardly any problems: birth rates being more or less stable, successive generations accumulated on a territory with a limited surplus until the demographic pressure became too great for the agricultural resources. Then regulative processes (famines and epidemics) were set in motion, bringing the population back to a level compatible with their resources.[20] The great novelty that emerged from the eighteenth century and was established by the middle of the nineteenth was to have overcome the 'natural' data of the problem by pushing back— and to what limits we still do not know today—the demographic burden that a society can support. The number of men ceased to be determined by the quantity of immediately available calories. This basic alteration in the fundamental factors of Western demography multiplied the number of labourers which, in turn, accelerated the process of industrialization because, in a system that had been centred upon economic efficiency ever since the eighteenth century, the multiplication of men multiplied opportunities, energies, the taste for risk-taking and enterprise, and also the chances for scientific and technical progress.[21] Thus, the quantity of labourers is no problem (in the medium and long term), even without making an appeal to the Marxist thesis of the industrial reserve army.

I have not said that demographic pressure determined the fundamental industrial change, but without it, it could not have been produced. If once more I were to indulge myself in comparative evidence, it would show that an increase in the number of men favours

[20] Under certain circumstances, for example, if prolonged wars add to the slaughter wrought by famine and plague, the decline may be such that the equilibrium is disturbed in an opposite direction and the number of men falls below the level required to make a given social system work. It took Germany nearly two centuries to recover after the Thirty Years War.

[21] It is impossible for me here to enter into controversies that, since Malthus, have shaken demography. It is important only to establish what appears to me to be a truth of the first order, that for two centuries the demographic explosion has been a consequence of the agricultural revolution and a powerful stimulus for the industrial revolution. The analyses of Alfred Sauvy have, on the other hand, shown that in an industrial system that gives itself economic growth as a primary objective, a continuous population increase remains indispensible, even today. Consequently, every programme of birth-control *in an industrial system* can only be based upon non-economic arguments.

capitalist activities. Thus the Tsing era in China, from the middle of the seventeenth century, experienced simultaneously a very marked demographic increase and an intensification of commercial trade. I have already noted what was probably a trebling of the Japanese population in the seventeenth century accompanied by a vigorous growth of capitalism. Inversely, a demographic decline, what the Ancients called oliganthropy, is followed by a fall in economic activity, as in Greece during the Hellenistic period or the late Roman Empire or in Spain from the seventeenth and eighteenth centuries.

The parallel between population and economic activity has something about it that is so evident and so necessary that one often forgets to account for it. If in fact I imagine easily enough that there is a direct link between demographic pressure on the one hand and land clearing, territorial expansion, an eagerness for war and military power or, beyond a certain threshold, scarcity, famine and epidemic, on the other, it does not seem to me that there is any direct link between demographic pressure and an increase in commercial trade. One must introduce mediations, reasoning something like as follows. In order for the great capitalist merchants to be employed there must be a demand for, and a supply of, luxury goods, or at least goods exceeding simple subsistence. Let us assume that there are no serious supply problems: if needs be one can have recourse to foreign suppliers. On the other hand, financially solvent demand is somewhat more problematic. So that it increases in an appreciable way, demand for luxury goods must increase. Now, three intelligible links between an increase in financially solvent demand and demographic pressure may be distinguished. In the first place, the State sees its fiscal resources increase: the expenses of the royal entourage and the public services increase as a result. Next, demographic pressure, in conformity to Ricardian theory, ends up increasing ground-rent by increasing the value of less fertile and productive land. Landlords see their revenues increase and will instigate a second demand for luxury goods. Finally, demographic pressure affects the division of land. The multiplication of men leads to a fragmentation of plots, and the smaller the size of a farm for a given level of agricultural technology, the greater the economic fragility since such farms will be more sensitive to climatic risks but will be without any reserves. It follows that the smaller and ruined farms must transfer their lands to the more fortunate and more competent. By and large demographic pressure must tend to eliminate middle-size farms and multiply both *minifundia*, too small to assure their owners of subsistence, and large properties developed in various ways (metayage, tenant farming, or large-scale farming using agricultural labourers) by the surplus members of second category.[22] Thus we may distinguish a third fiscally solvent demand, that of the large farmers. To summarize: demographic pressure in an agrarian system will have a tendency to increase the revenues of the governors and their henchmen, the landlords and the large farmers. In economic terms, one would speak of an increase of rents and profits. It is the increase in these revenues that determines the demand for luxury goods and provides the occasion for merchant activity. *But* it is clear that, in the absence of a basic change in agricultural technology, demographic pressure cannot exceed a certain threshold without activating compensatory moments. The great innovation of the eighteenth, and especially the nineteenth, century was to have broken the circle. Consequently, if demographic pressure is a stimulus for capitalist activity, it is outside its power to instigate a decisive rupture of the economic system and effect a passage to industrial capitalism.

In this way the West had labourers available in sufficient numbers. In addition, it was necessary that these labourers had the qualities required by an industrial system namely, as I have already said, an ability to change their qualifications and a willingness to work. The first point is connected with the extension of instruction to the lower levels of society. It would be wrong to argue that the transmission of knowledge to everyone, beginning with the most elementary matters of reading, writing, and arithmetic, was undertaken for reasons of economic Machiavellianism. The explanation is at once moral and political. Universal instruction has become a major demand because, since the Renaissance, elites have developed an ideology that based all good things upon knowledge and because, since the French Revolution, the West has been seized with the vertigo of equality. Universal instruction was first of all applied to primary education then secondary education before, in our own day, having overtaken the universities. Once again the cunning of western history has diverted this fine project to the benefit of the economy. In fact, the more the labourer is broadened intellectually, the more he can learn to learn, and the more easily he can adapt himself to the transformations of the economic system. As always, consciousness is behind reality, and it took one or two decades for this phenomenon to be put voluntarily to the service

[22] Emmanuel LeRoy-Ladurie has followed this process step by step in Languedoc: *Les Paysans de Languedoc* (Paris: Flammarion, 1969).

of the economy, leading to the present educational crises we all know about. The ability to change qualifications is most important for the industrial system, and it depends upon instruction.[23] It is not the only factor. Geographical mobility clearly plays a role. In fact, the more an active population is disposed to change its residence in order to adapt to the variations in economic circumstances, the more flexible and efficient the system will be. In the lands of European colonization such as North America and Australia the absence of any archaic peasant and provincial roots (particularly strong in France) facilitates the movement of people and removes one source of rigidity from the system.

Willingness to work brings us back to problems of psychology. Tristan Bernard's celebrated caprice contains a deeper philosophical insight: man is not made for labour, and his natural inclination is to do as little as possible.

Thus, he must have good reason to raise himself to it. The methods that man has perfected to compel labour may all be reduced to three principal types. The least efficient is violence, that is, forced labour imposed permanently upon a fraction of the population (slaves, prisoners). This method is the least efficient, I say, because of the considerable restraints it demands and the great cost of surveillance and organization it brings with it. The most efficient is enthusiasm. That is, the voluntary gift of one's strength and time in order to accomplish a collective task. This is rather an idealistic method, for human societies having to date always been hierarchical, and enthusiasm would primarily benefit the higher levels, which would reduce its chances of happening. The rare examples that may be observed are tied to exceptional circumstances (periods of war or revolution), which are by nature transitory. And, there is the last method: the necessity of meeting wants.

There are no natural or elementary wants or demands. Rather, what passes for elementary are what a given society considers to be so. Versailles could be considered in certain respects as an elementary demand for absolute monarchy. Even the simple satisfaction of alimentary needs may take an infinity of forms, given that, up to the present, no collectivity has been content simply to swallow down calories. Consequently, the more a society diversifies and multiplies the goods that can be the object of a desire, the more demands, which are unlimited by nature, since they are limited by culture, will increase. The

[23] Cf. Edward F. Denison, *Why Growth Rates Differ: Postwar Experience in Nine Western Countries* (Washington: Brookings Institution, 1967), ch. 8.

H

result is the necessity to ensure that these wants and consequently this labour, are proportional to desires. Thus there is no mystery in the disagreeable fact that, to the degree that humanity increases its dominion over nature and increases its technology of production, it adds, at the same time, to the number of hours devoted to labour. Labourers and consumers are synonymous. Consequently, the real reason why the industrial system found the labourers it needed was the liberation of demand. The real logic of the system is not at all as Marx thought nor as some of his later followers still think, the impoverishment and enslavement of large numbers of people, but rather the production of greater numbers of ever more prosperous consumers.

Granted that the liberation of demand always pushes the point of satisfaction farther away and thus, at the same time, adds to dissatisfaction,[24] the tendency is still towards the liberation of demand. Yet, must not this tendency be thwarted? In fact, like all human activity, the demands a society recognizes as elementary (and the needs that the several social categories of this society so recognize) tend to form a system and thus to limit themselves. What is considered as an elementary want will depend upon the way of life involved: for a wretch in the slums of Calcutta, a Cadillac is not desirable and cannot be experienced as a demand. In the same way, the enjoyment of a Chateau in the Loire Valley is beyond the middle-class Frenchman. The genesis of demand in western capitalism is identified with the dissolution of traditional ways of life. For nearly a thousand years the whole evolution of the West has been in this direction. Political factors are, once again, of the first importance. The creation of larger and larger political units from the eleventh century on has tended to suppress the barriers between the upper classes of Western society. The wants of the nobility and the upper bourgeoisie were rapidly liberated and transformed by a frenzy of luxury purchases, which served to benefit the development of the major and minor arts, at least up to the eighteenth century. Wars, rendered inevitable by coexistence within the same cultural space of several political units, multiplied contacts and so also multiplied demand (consider the consequences of the Italian wars for the construction of French chateaux). And finally, the great voyages of exploration and especially the various colonization activities put the West into contact with a multitude of ways of life or demand-systems.

[24] For a more comprehensive analysis of this point, see the book of my friend, Pierre Kende, *L'Abondance, est-elle possible?* (Paris: Gallimard, 1971) esp. the second part.

In this way the traditional Western ways of life lost their seeming necessity and could be easily dismantled, thereby opening Pandora's box. The internal revolution of the West was in the same direction: urbanization, the concentration of men within reduced spaces, internal migration—all these changes broke down the isolation of ways of life and liberated demand.[25] There is no need to insist upon this for it is all quite plain. And so I have a fourth point to add to my model: an elastic consumer, able to absorb all kinds of innovations. No doubt the elasticity is imperfect, for restraints inevitably reappear: the unlimited power of advertising over the consumer is a myth dear to the hearts of peculiar proletaroid intellectuals (the expression is Max Weber's), but it is only a myth.

[25] Cooking and dietary systems could be the object of a fascinating study: how limited but coherent regional cooking has been transformed into an international but eccentric and incongruous cuisine.

Ten: *The Contemporary Basis of the Capitalist Spirit*

It is not enough simply to have set forth the origins of a social system. It is still necessary to show why it endures or, to use more precise terms, to show how every new generation is made to assimilate the values that society holds out to it. When a society is stable, the question poses no difficulty, for the possibilities of deviation from the received model are very slight. On the other hand, Western civilization finds its fundamental characteristic, as I hope to have shown, in the absence of order and in the constant changes that result.

As a consequence, the integration of the young is not automatically accomplished and the industrial spirit must be re-born with each generation; eventually it must be based on new foundations. It would take me too far afield to inquire upon all the present-day foundations of the industrial spirit, and I would like to suggest only those that seem to me essential: the political, the cultural, and the ideological. I must be content with a few general indications, for my venture is drawing to a close and I am entering unknown waters.

1. *Politics and the Economy.* In its most general sense, politics may be defined as the human activity by which a group ensures internal harmony and external security. Now, these two exigencies have invariable economic consequences. Internally, the tendency to transform all labourers into wage-labourers (one of the characteristics of the industrial system) presents the problem of re-dividing national revenue in increasingly conflict-centred terms. In fact, the portion that goes to each group of wage-labourers is determined by the portions of all the

others. Within a system where the supreme value is held to be an increase in one's standard of living, economic stagnation means an exacerbation of conflicts as each individual can only increase his own portion to the detriment of others. In order to maintain harmony political power is condemned to favour economic expansion by any available means. To-day in order to survive there is no political regime that is not obliged to undertake a policy of growth. Now, growth is based upon increasing productivity, which is to say, upon the necessity constantly to eliminate a fraction of labourers from the production system. As wages tend to be the sole source of revenue, unemployment is the supreme catastrophy for the individual. But this unemployment is inevitable if the economic system is constantly to grow. The necessity of ensuring internal harmony thus once more condemns political power to a course of expansion. We must add a third reason: demographic increase. The West, and following it, other contemporary civilizations have not yet succeeded in attaining their demographic equilibrium—so much so, in fact, that the increase in the number of men also makes economic expansion indispensable.

The necessity of ensuring external security reinforces this tendency. It is clear that the weight of a political unit on the international scene depends upon the material and human forces it has available for mobilization in case of conflict. Whether the orientation of government is offensive or defensive, security will only be assured if economic might permits the creation of an armament system at least equal to that of the strongest enemy.[26]

War has always been the most favoured means of establishing a hierarchy among political units. It is not the only one: prestige has also always played a role. In our time, the pursuit of prestige leads to economic consequences; material or technical aid, technological exploits, etc. (it is difficult to explain space exploration, colour television, supersonic aeroplanes and so forth in any other way). To claim to play a role on the international scene presupposes a certain amount of industrial strength. The experience of the U.S.S.R. proves that a totalitarian power may clear the threshold of international power provided it has sufficient size and human and material resources, and

[26] The example of Viet-Nam and, in general, guerilla warfare would seem to weaken this law. But only in appearance. In fact, the guerilla is victorious only if he succeeds in mobilizing the whole population. Atomic genocide would get rid of him. Consequently, the guerilla is effective only so long as his adversary excludes total annihilation from the field of possible strategies.

does not count the human and economic cost of rapid industrialization. But industrial *strength* is not synonymous with industrial society.[27] It is not enough just to produce guns; simultaneously it is necessary to produce butter. An industrial society means the systematic search for economic efficiency in all directions, including private consumption. The Soviet experience shows simply that by paying the price, by neglecting consumer demand, and by copying others, one can build up a heavy industry so as to attain military strength in spite of numerous infractions of all the laws of economics.

In the under-developed countries the economic consequences of every political policy are even plainer. At the level of greatest abstraction, under-development may be defined as the rupture of traditional equilibria (biological, economic, political, and psychological) as a result of contact with the West. The results are most striking at the demographic and economic levels. The situation is so dramatic that the leaders of these countries cannot avoid advertising that their most important concerns have to do with economic growth. It may be doubted whether they always—or even predominantly—employ the most rational means to attain it. In fact, the two main features of the 'third world', namely nationalist excitement and state direction of the economy, necessarily have negative consequences for economic growth. The Cuban and Guinean experience, to cite only the most resounding failures, provide a fairly complete catalogue of what must be done to be sure of ruining an economy. But that is a different problem. What remains true is that the search for growth, which began as a European accident has become an obligatory command for the Whole World.

2. *The cultural aspect.* The Western spirit has tended for a thousand years to introduce change in every area. I have tried to show that this spirit must become bound to political pluralism, both internally and externally. The social system established on these foundations is the first that has ceased to root itself in a single interpretation of the human condition but has established itself on the basis of *experimentation*. In all these areas—political, economic, religious, scientific, ethical, aesthetic—the West has for centuries given itself up to experiments, as if it were meaning to survey the whole field of possibilities available for the human adventure. For the first time, tradition is seen if not as an evil, at least as a deficiency. Change in itself has become a value. This is

[27] I borrow this apposite distinction from Annie Kriegel.

painfully obvious in the artistic realm where the first quality required of a painter is not to paint like anyone else. Imitation or simply the fact of holding to a current or a tradition are seen as deficiencies. The result is that the obsolescence of objects, goods, institutions, and ideas ceaselessly accelerates and is experienced as a progress. Everyone claims to be revolutionary and cheerfully harries every vestige of stability. To claim to be a conservative is the surest way to find oneself classified with the fossils. It is remarkable that despite the discomforts and sufferings that follow from such an orientation, capitalist society has succeeded in producing in increasing numbers individuals who have adapted morally to a way of life whose breathless rhythms result from the absence of any profound ones. It is possible that we may be on the brink of a reversal of this orientation, or at least a questioning of its merits.

3. *An Ideological Factor.* It is probable that the moving idea of western society for the past two centuries has been equality. Now this passion inevitably moves in the direction of accentuating economic activities. If, in the eighteenth century, equality was a vague demand, a simple opposition to the nobility (for example in *The Marriage of Figaro*), with the French Revolution it became a political exigency, a will to transform all the members of a nation into citizens capable of participating actively in group objectives. Inevitably this exigency must reach the economy.[28] After some early incoherence, which made economic inequality depend upon inequality of distribution and thus on property, economic thought eventually had to arrive at the retrospective awareness that, in the final analysis, inequality proceeds from scarcity. In a realm of scarcity, the distribution of goods is made in terms of relations of force (whose determination is, nevertheless, complex). From this, two and only two solutions are logically possible:

(a) *The elimination of relations of force,* which is to say, the constitution of a society without politics. Inevitably here one ends up in a system of self-management. The difficulty is that the ideologues of self-management seem to forget that this result only makes sense if it ends scarcity not by absolute abundance, which is an absurdity, but by the limitation of demand. That is, it presupposes the establishment of a civilization and a stable order and assumes a human nature that would be satisfied by uniformity of conditions. One may remain sceptical when one recalls

[28] For several years now we have been in an ultimate phase, that of equality of intellectual culture.

that in all known societies a basic tendency for all individuals is to distinguish themselves. It needs more than a generous utopia to convince us that the social comedy that Veblen so acidly depicted is nought but an historical accident, and not deeply rooted in the heart of man.

(b) *The elimination, pure and simple, of scarcity.* This is the myth of abundance that has been reverberating in our ears for two decades. Without entering into the details of this ideological drollery, let us simply note that abundance is an inconsistent concept. It would indicate a condition where goods exceeded desires, which is logically absurd since desires are not rooted in human nature but defined simply by the desires of others. Thus they are by nature infinite.[29] Even under the unsustainable hypothesis that natural resources were unlimited, the state of abundance is ceaselessly pushed farther and farther away by the concomitant development of desires. All the same, for the time being this ideology seems to hold sway and consequently to entail the constant development of production. Thus it is at one with the simple exigencies of internal politics, namely the maintenance of harmony within the social body. I would not say that the ideology is only a mask for practical politics (a politics beyond economics), but that the two orientations are convergent even though they have different origins.

I have tried to restrain the scope of these few remarks only so as to fill in the score of western particularities and to understand the kinds of sentiments they inspire. The capitalist adventure has induced both enthusiasm and hatred. The enthusiasm may be a result of the striking material and intellectual success it has attained. Here it is comparable to no other similar feat in any civilization. It is sustained by the conviction that its success has allowed it to extend its influence over the whole world, whether directly by conquest or by foreign adoption of Western models. It is convinced that the movement has barely begun and that a general welfare may be anticipated. The hatred of capitalism has only inconvenienced the choice of arguments. They may be classified into two general categories. One can insist upon the costs of this success and show that it is accompanied by as much destruction: age-old ways of life destroyed by an arrogant morality of efficiency, natural and social orders of an incontestable value, stability and permanence that is certainly more in conformity with human nature than incessant change—all these things have gone. Indeed, each of us could

[29] A remarkable analysis of desire may be found in a work of René Girard, *Deceit, Desire and the Novel: Self and Other in Literary Structure*, tr. Y. Freccero (Baltimore: Johns Hopkins University Press, 1965).

easily draw up an inexhaustible catalogue of the inconveniences of economic growth. A second approach seeks to show the intrinsic absurdity of the capitalist system. What kind of civilization is it whose ultimate goal is an annual growth rate of 5 per cent (or 3 per cent or 10 per cent)? To put the question so bluntly leads necessarily to emphasize other possible values and other (religious, military, political, playful) objects of inspiration.

Criticism of the capitalist system is easy enough for anyone to do it. To propose a solution that does not at the same time involve the disappearance of goods that everyone thinks worthwhile is quite another question. I make no claims in this direction; I do not seek to turn myself into a prophet for a better society. Another position seems to me to be more interesting and more in agreement with the vocation of a scholar. Starting from the criticisms just mentioned, and assuming them to be well-founded (or that some groups think they are, which amounts to the same thing), what are the reactions they create and threaten to create? If it is true that the West has had a tendency to exalt economic activities, then by what detour, in what forms, and with what success will other values again attain prominence? What models of society are possible, and capable of mobilizing energy and people? If it is true that, beyond a certain threshold, cultural pluralism is irreversible and self-sustaining, can the social contract still be upheld? Are there other ways to maintain the cohesion of a society than consensus, brute force, and hatred of others? The answer to these and other similar questions constitutes the best scientific analysis of the contemporary West. My deepest feeling is that, for a thousand years, the West has been the privileged centre of fundamental changes, of revolutions, and the most daring experiments in all realms of life; in achieving these, it has given the human adventure dimensions undreamed of anywhere else. Its diversity and instability have been tied to its political pluralism and one can not hope to get rid of the manifestations of pluralism without destroying pluralism itself. These are the freedoms upon which the greatness of the West is based, and they have imposed a heavy burden upon it, for freedom rests upon an exacting self-mastery. It is not at all certain that the vast number of men would aspire to it but would not rather prefer subjection.

Conclusion

I think I have resolved the problem I set for myself and have found the reasons for the appearance of capitalism in the West. The argument I have followed is based upon the series of interconnected propositions that follows:

1. The specific feature that belongs only to the capitalist system is the privileged position accorded the search for economic efficiency.
2. The first condition for the maximization of economic efficiency is the liberation of civil society with respect to the State.
3. This condition is fulfilled when a single cultural area is divided into several sovereign political units.
4. So that all these potential factors lead to all their consequences, it is also necessary that the value-system be modified to the detriment of religious, military and political values, and that demand be liberated.
5. Only the West has experienced an evolution where all these conditions were met. The feudal order resulting from the decline of the western provinces of the Roman Empire paid no attention to trade. When trade reappeared it produced an original being, the bourgeois, devoted to economic tasks but stripped of all social legitimacy. The absence of a European political order led to the anarchy of the market and the impossibility of creating an economic order. The devaluation of religious, political and military functions concentrated men's energies on economic activities. And finally, the destruction of traditional ways of life liberated demand and produced the modern consumer.

Conclusion

The same line of argument allows us to explain why the industrial revolution took place in England at the end of the eighteenth century. Up to now it has been enough to take note of the fact or to credit it to certain specific features clearly tied to the phenomenon to be explained. For example, the increased demand for cotton goods required an increase in weaving, from which came the adoption of improved looms. Then a bottleneck appeared in spinning and the spinning machine came along, and so on. My hypothesis emphasizes the fact that the pluralist English system was firmly in place by the eighteenth century, that, after centuries of internal and foreign wars, Europe arrived at a long period of political stability, that States had become unified by an efficient administration, that from the time of Newton, the scientific spirit had made great strides in England, and that the English elite was more concerned with the economy than with military or political opportunities. I think that the proof is clear enough and that there was nothing miraculous about the English advance. Having said that, we must add that the whole European system was favourable to the blossoming of the industrial system. This is why it encountered no serious problems when it spread to France, Holland, Belgium, Germany, Northern Italy and Bohemia. If the eighteenth century (and following it, even more surely in the nineteenth century after the interludes of the French Revolution and the Napoleonic Empire—and for the same reasons) for the first time realized all the conditions posed in my argument, it is also clear that one must go back to the eleventh century to grasp the progressive genesis of these conditions.

Every argument such as I have followed in this essay is based on a definition and an assumption. The *definition* delimits the object of the explanation. It follows that every definition, because it is arbitrary, is open to debate. However, it seems to me that the definition I ended up adopting allows for the best interpretation of the facts. Having said that, it follows that if one were looking for the origins of the English system during the Victorian age or the origins of the Welfare State, the explanation would have to take account of more minute factual data. I only hope that the conclusions of such an investigation would not contradict the main features of my argument. The *assumption* may be expressed as follows: from the moment there appeared an animal endowed with speech and capable of using his arm as a tool, a field of possibilities was outlined within which the capitalist system may be found. My whole effort has been to establish why the West grasped this opportunity. My answer is that the ultimate cause must be sought in *i.e., too much aggression to enable an Empire to be formed.*

the coexistence of severe political units in the same cultural area. I have constantly insisted upon the fortuitous nature of this evolution: capitalism was no more on the horizon of Antiquity than it was on the horizon of China during the Han period. But it was just as much. Consequently, one may legitimately wonder if capitalism would not have appeared on the earth anyhow, even if the specific data of western history were different. No rigorous answer may be given to such a question. I would say simply this: capitalism being a possibility ever since the paleolithic age, the multiplicity and diversity of cultures that have developed on the earth make it highly probable that one of them one day would end up seizing this possibility.

Every philosophy of history that is based on the idea of a linear and necessary evolution seems to me to be at once false and uninteresting. It is uninteresting because it rests upon a *petitio principii*, namely that the only possible history is the one that in fact resulted. To declare the necessity of one outcome is only to avow one's inability to explore other possibilities. It is false because it is constantly contradicted by facts. Human societies are not swept along by a destiny greater than they, a destiny impossible to grasp. For thousands of years they have been given over to experiences crowned with both success and failure. Gradually, and in addition to all these experiences, a field of possibility may be discerned and then consciously grasped. The work of science consists in making clear the circumstances and the reasons whereby one possibility is achieved. Now—and, if this essay has any merit, it is this—the least hazardous method consists in comparison. It allows us gradually to determine the variables pertinent to the phenomenon under study by grasping their differences. For capitalism, the significant variable appears to be politics. Contrary to nearly universal opinion, the social sciences do not seem to me to be inferior to the natural sciences simply because they are unable to perform experiments. It is enough to start from the hypothesis that human history is a gigantic laboratory, where experiments are permanently going on, in order to seek to isolate these experiments and ask oneself about the laws which they might verify. The succession of operations is the opposite to what obtains in the natural sciences, but that changes nothing of the effectiveness of the experimental method one way or another. In fact, the great difference and the major difficulty of the social sciences consists in the impossibility of isolating the phenomena without multiplying them too much. It is possible and even probable that human societies are concrete totalities. But, they can only be grasped by an understanding condemned to more or less distorted reconstructions. In this essay I have not presented the infinite complexity of the reality that I have called the capitalist system. I have been able to deal only with a limited aspect of it. Others who are better qualified would no doubt have done better; no one can recover the totality.